P

Energy Teachings of the Three

"Profound and timely insights and practices for these turbulent times. The world needs this!"

—**Alberto Villoldo**,
author of *Shaman, Healer, Sage,* and founder of the Four Winds Society

"Humanity faces a challenging future. The problems around us and ahead of us are not unresolvable, but to resolve them, we need to reach into resources of spirit and life, the wellsprings of wholeness that are innate within us but so often untapped. We are not just physical bodies but beings of spirit and energy as well. Discovering and applying this truth is the true challenge of the future. This wonderful book by David Kyle provides clear and powerful tools to meet this challenge and unlock the powerful resources within us."

—**David Spangler**,
author of *Working with Subtle Energies*

"All of us long for a download of divine wisdom, a perspective on our lives that springs from a source beyond our ordinary awareness. David Kyle received just that while he was on a retreat, from three beings who delivered a life-changing revelation. Their words and David's ongoing communication with the Three reveal a vastly expanded view of our human journey, one that transcends time and space, and makes complete awakening inevitable. Their teachings on love, appreciation, compassion, kindness, gratitude, and forgiveness reflect the essence of the perennial philosophy that underlies every spiritual path. But rather than just offering ideas, this book gives us concrete practices that allow us to apply these concepts in everyday life. You're likely to feel these transformational currents infusing your own heart and body as you immerse yourself in the information field carried by this precious book."

—**Dawson Church**,
award-winning author of *Bliss Brain: The Neuroscience of Remodeling Your Brain for Resilience, Creativity and Joy*

"David writes beautifully and articulately in *Energy Teachings of the Three*, a book expressing profound truths that wisdom traditions have been pointing to for millennia. Through David's transcriptions of the teachings of the Three, this book offers key practices on appreciation, compassion, forgiveness, kindness, and gratitude that can help awaken you to the transformational power of love in all its forms."

—**Mark Coleman**,
author of *From Suffering to Peace*

"David Kyle is a brilliant teacher and shamanic practitioner who has provided me with invaluable counsel, guidance, and mentoring over the years. His new, channeled book is called *Energy Teachings of the Three*. It is an energetic guidebook for the tumultuous times we are living in today. David teaches us about the five pillars of love and shares psycho-spiritual practices that will help you expand the power of love and connection in your life. He shares invaluable practices for grounding our heart energy in solid, practical, and accessible ways to meet the fear, frustration, and fragmentation that appear to be escalating in our world today. David's positive approach to personal and planetary healing is a huge contribution to the evolution of the human species."

—**Michael Stone**,
author, teacher, and radio host

"This is a beautiful work of rich origin and great destiny. Many will come to drink at this well and be nourished."

—**Don Hynes**,
poet, author of *The Irish Girl*

"This book is one of the greatest gifts I have been given. It will take the rest of this life to fully engrain these steps into my being—and what a blessing that is!"

—**Marlene Bottenfield**,
University teacher, motivational speaker

"*Energy Teachings of the Three* is a timely testament that will provide step-by-step guidance for the spiritual seeker wanting to evolve the new human(ity). The depth of the material delivers ancient wisdom and yet it is presented in simple and understandable segments that offer insightful daily practices. A must-have for your spiritual books shortlist."

—**Rev. Jerry Farrell**,
co-author of *Keeping the Promise*

"I cannot praise this book enough. I highly recommended it for everyone who has embarked upon the path of expanded consciousness. Having received an advanced copy from the author as an early draft, I have been using and integrating the teachings of the Three into my own personal practice for a few years now, as well as introducing them to my clients and students with powerful results. Given the present chaotic state of the world, this is a timely and much-needed guidebook. I believe that if you do nothing else in the way of daily practice, consistent use of this material will expand your perception and accelerate your spiritual evolution enormously, no matter how 'woke' you think you are. This deceptively simple book will take you to a new level of awareness and show you how you to practice the highest form of activism: self-transformation."

—**Jim 'Redtail' Collins, PhD**,
Eco-therapist and shamanic teacher at
Mountain Rising: School for a New Way of Being

ENERGY TEACHINGS
of
The Three

ENERGY TEACHINGS
of
The Three

Guidance and Practices to Open
Your Heart and Heal Your Mind

David Kyle, PhD

Dancing Raven & Company

Copyright © 2021 by David T. Kyle

All rights reserved. This book or any portion thereof may not be reproduced or used in any manner whatsoever without the express written permission of the publisher except for the use of brief quotations in a book review or scholarly journal.

Published by Dancing Raven & Company
Nevada City, CA
www.davidkylenc.com

First Printing: 2021

Editor: Nina Shoroplova—ninashoroplova.ca
Cover Design: Pagatana Design Service—www.pagatana.com
Book Interior and E-book Design: Amit Dey—amitdey2528@gmail.com
Production & Publishing Consultant: Geoff Affleck—geoffaffleck.com

Library of Congress Number: 2020921850

ISBN: 978-1-7361066-0-0 (p)
ISBN: 978-1-7361066-2-4 (e)

OCC003000 BODY, MIND & SPIRIT / Channeling & Mediumship
OCC011000 BODY, MIND & SPIRIT / Healing / General
OCC011010 BODY, MIND & SPIRIT / Healing / Energy
OCC019000 BODY, MIND & SPIRIT / Inspiration & Personal Growth
OCC036030 BODY, MIND & SPIRIT / Shamanism

Dedication

To my teachers and guides, friends and family who have accompanied me on my life journey. Thank you for your Love and kindness.

Contents

The Source of the Energy Teachings.............................. 1

The Five Pillars of Love 11

    Appreciation 15

    Compassion.. 19

    Forgiveness 25

    Kindness 31

    Gratitude 35

    Implications of the Five Pillars Practices 41

    Crossing the Threshold: Practicing the Five Pillars of Love 45

The Five Foundation Stones for Daily Living 49

    Self-Love... 55

    Humility... 59

    Self-Acceptance 65

    Reflection.. 73

    Release of Old Patterns..................................... 79

    Working with Your Practice 87

The Challenges of the End Times 91
The Nature of Times Ahead 95
The Meaning of the Planet's Environmental Changes 103
The Spiritual Meaning of Ending and Beginnings 111
The Promise of a New World, a New Pattern of Living, and the Awakening of the Truly Human 121
Afterword 135
Acknowledgement 139
About the Author 141

The Source
of the Energy Teachings

Throughout my life, I've had a strong affinity to ancient shamanic and extra-dimensional experiences. I've had both physical and extra-dimensional teachers who have assisted me in my life journey. This book is a recording of one of these extraordinary experiences that was a significant part of my shamanic training in Peru.

In the early 2000s, I began to learn and practice the Andean healing tradition. The particular path was that of the Laika from the Q'ero tradition of the high Andean Mountains. In addition to my teachers in North America, I have two teachers in Peru who provided initiations, teachings, and practices for my mental, emotional, physical, and spiritual development. One of my teachers, a Peruvian *Paqo* (meaning "sacred person"), had been working with me in a number of sacred sites over several days to prepare me for an initiation in a sacred cave. The intent of the initiation was for me to experience the intense energy of the cave and the inherent power of being initiated as a significant step in my training.

The cave was high up above a river bed. To get to the cave we hiked up a steep ancient staircase on the side of a mountain. Looked at from far below, the cave opening appeared to be a perfect triangle. The use of the cave by humans is considered pre-Incan and the site may be ten thousand or more years old. Inside the cave at its entrance is a carved throne-like altar. Farther into the cave (that structurally is a huge equilateral triangle) and carved out of the rock is a long wall with an inset seat. The throne altar and the thirty-foot wall are perfectly straight and smooth as though someone used a laser cutter to carve out a throne with three seats and an angled sloping cave wall. This wall is seven feet high by thirty feet long. In its center is a square sitting space, measuring three feet wide by four feet high and a couple of feet deep. The ceiling of this triangular cave extends up thirty or forty feet at the peak. The cave reaches back approximately seventy-five feet with offering niches built into the rock sides for ceremony.

Energetically, just stepping into the cave was very powerful. My body prickled with energy as though an electrical charge radiated all over my body.

After describing the purpose of the cave, my teacher had me sit in the middle chair of the "throne altar" and close my eyes. The initiation was very simple. He spritzed me in the belly, heart, and head with Florida water (Florida Water is a face lotion used in Peru by shamans for the purpose of purifying the energy field of the body), laid his hands on my head, and spoke words over me in Quechua (the native language of the Andes).

My eyes were closed as he stepped away from me.

Suddenly, I felt a bolt of energy run from my head down to the base of my spine. As the energy surged inside me, the image of three very elongated bodies between seven and eight feet tall appeared before me. Together they approached me and touched my belly, heart, and head. I knew their touching me to be a blessing and again I felt an incredible energy run up my body from the base of my spine to the top of my head. The movement of energy down through and up my spine seemed to both cauterize and open my body, as well as my heart and mind.

After I sat deeper inside the cave for a while, absorbing the energy from the three beings, my teacher had me sit in the square niche in the center of the wall. Here he did another part of the initiation, blowing smoke from a handmade cigar into my head, heart, and belly. He then taught me how to experience myself outside of time. He told me that this initiation was to take me through the tear in time and space to experience a dimension beyond this one. In experiencing that part of the initiation, I saw elements of my past, present, and future. During the rest of the day, as I absorbed this heightened energy awareness, I had visual flashes of people and events appearing before me in different time and space environments. For example, the teacher's seven-year-old son was with us and I saw him at one point twenty years in the future. Another student was with us and I saw mixed elements of spatial and temporal changes in her life, which ranged from her past to her future as well as a kind of prophecy of what was emerging for her at that time in her life pattern.

Later, upon leaving the cave and returning to his house, my teacher told me that his teacher had initiated him in the cave and he too had experienced the three beings. He urged me to find a way to communicate with these three beings. He said that he would not say more about them, but he did say this: "You need to find a way of relating with them. They are now your teachers for this time on your journey."

He would not speak to me any more about them, even when I would ask questions. He simply would shake his head, "no."

With that I explored various means to communicate with them.

In the days and months that followed this initiation I found that I could engage in communication with the three beings through a question-and-answer method of writing that continues to this day. I've asked a vast array of questions about them, where they came from, the nature of the universe, our world today, and my own challenges and directions for my life.

Many times when I would pose a question, they would disregard it and instead give me information on practices for working with energy and frequency patterns to open and transform my mind and heart. Much of the information has been personal to my wife and me, but clearly they want the information they gave me on Love and the energy practices to be shared with a larger audience.

Through this communication with them, I learned the names of the "Three," as they call themselves. They gave me their individual names as Jaybar, Raymar, and Kandin. They told me that these names are the approximate representation of the language they spoke thousands of years ago, but that their language was tonal and would be difficult to comprehend. I was told that Kandin teaches about energy, Jaybar teaches about information, and Raymar presents the vast nature of how energy frequencies function throughout the multi-dimensional universes.

I learned much later after returning to the United States why these beings came to me as three rather than as just one being. There is a long history of threes in mythology, the mystical traditions, and in the history of religion. In the ancient goddess traditions, for example, there are the maiden, mother, and crone. There are the three graces, the three muses, the three-headed goddess Hecate. And there is also the god represented in many ancient cultures with three heads: one faces forward and the other two to each side. In Greek and Roman mythology, there is the three-headed dog of Hades called Cerberus, which represents past, present, and future, and guards the entrance to the underworld.

The Three hold this same mythic triad.

I realized recently, after thinking about the Three, that they once told me: "We three are really one being providing different facets to the sources of life and energy." The Three said that they came to me in the space/time cave to teach me how to view the past, present, and future outside of time. The Three appear to hold a vast sweep of time and space not only of this Universe, but of multiple Universes.

What follows is a transcription of the information they have provided to me on the Five Pillars of Love, the Five Foundation Stones for Daily Living, and the Challenges of the End Times.

Raymar describes their role with me in the following way:

> We came to you in Peru in the space/time cave to initiate you into something that has been part of you for many years. Together we are a teaching unit. Kandin will tell you more about his role, but together we act as one unit. When Jaybar spoke to you about

heart frequency we all three were speaking to you. We are really one mind connected to the Universal Mind. You could say that we are three facets of one gem nested into a multitude of gems. If one of us seems to speak to you, in reality all of us are. *As we speak in your mind and as you write, we access your word structure, concepts, knowledge, and information as well as your own style of communication. If you have difficulty understanding what we are placing in your mind, ask a question, and we will respond in a different manner.*

Now, we each have a particular form of information to give to you. Mine is the understanding of the vast nature of energy. Your scientists are being taught about different forms of energy by many other intelligences who inhabit similar dimensions that we inhabit and who are like us. Most of these scientists are not in direct communication with these intelligences but are having the information placed in their minds.

We are from the ancient civilization many people call Mu or Lemuria. Our civilization was destroyed as the earth plates tore apart the earth and our land was buried in what is now the far west of the Pacific Ocean. However, Lemuria was not the name we gave it. There is great misunderstanding about our civilization because a significant part of our development was not on the surface of the planet. Rather we understood the inter-dimensional nature of energy and we learned to live outside of time and space. In fact, we are still living in this manner. We are coming to you in this moment from the energy realm called the dimension of pure light. Many inter-dimensional beings have "lived" around this earth planet for millions of years just as they live around many other planets throughout multiple universes. Three-dimensional beings like yourself who have experienced the so-called UFO experience are actually experiencing beings from non-space-and-time dimensions as they manifest into your time and space.

We now exist in a rich and vibrant multi-dimensionality and are able to move throughout the complex of universes, exploring and learning. Thus, we have contact with many other types of intelligences throughout the many dimensions of what you think of as reality. We are here to help mitigate and focus the appropriate connections of these beings to you. We helped you with this when you had the inter-dimensional contact for ten years and you identified that contact with what you termed a bio signal.

(From my mid-twenties to mid-thirties, I experienced contact with beings in another dimension. That is another story.)

We also helped bring that work to a conclusion so you could move forward to integrate and develop your conscious awareness more fully on your own. Those beings who were in contact with you then helped you to broaden your perception, break down the walls of your beliefs, and helped you come to trust yourself.

Remember, the number one imperative in existence is to grow and transform. The experience of three-dimensional birth and death is a very different matter than what your previous experiences have been in other dimensions of reality. In this dimension as a human it is a process of awakening your consciousness to perceive beyond the normal conditioning of this particular pattern of reality you live within.

In this life you have a number of teachers and guides from other realms. You are a unit with them. Just as we three are a unit. You can remember that each one came to you at a particular time for your awareness and development. You help and serve each of them just as they do the same for you. It is Love and energy that lets you grow together. What we understand about Love is that it is the most basic energy form *in the Universe.*

Your scientists have broken energy down to the smallest particles. They have learned—among other characteristics—how these particles interact in attraction to each other and how they appear and disappear. All that your scientists are "discovering" is just one level of this energy called Love. One can work with, learn from, and have direct experience of various types of energy, but the most universal energy is Love. What you have been learning about the fundamental principle of Love energy is basic to your life. As you will soon come to know through these energy practices, *the basic foundations of Love are appreciation, compassion, forgiveness, kindness, gratitude.* Each of these words represents different energy aspects of Love. We will show you more about each of these principles as energy forms that transform reality.

Go now and have your morning walk. It is good to connect with you.

> **What we understand about Love is that it is the most basic energy form in the Universe.**

First Comment

The communication with the Three about the nature of Love and energy developed through my asking questions and the Three "dictating" their responses to me. My experience of contact with them came primarily in written form.

Sometimes without asking a question I would experience them communicating directly into my mind. The dictations had the quality of automatic writing, in the sense that the words would come into my mind before I could write them down. If I had to stop writing for some reason, I could stop and start the dictation, and it would easily start again in the same place in the communication. I was generally surprised by the vocabulary and the information of which I had no personal knowledge.

In one session I was curious about their present experience, the dimension that they operate within, and the reason they were communicating with me. I asked them, "What dimension are you in as we communicate?"

> We are in the fifth dimension. When we lived in what you call Lemuria, we had learned to transform ourselves to be able to move back and forth from the third dimension to the fifth. In reality, we are present in both time and space as well as in the realm of light, which is the fifth dimension. We can move beyond the fifth but to be in contact with you we resume the energy of the fifth. All your guides come from the fifth as well. This is the dimension we can take on forms that you can relate to.

> In Peru we appeared as tall, elongated beings because that is what those who have contact with us in the cave have seen projected as our form. Your teacher in Peru received the same initiation as you. There are others of our community who are also teachers for him. This is why he could confirm your experience with us. In Peru we have had an affinity to the space/time cave long before the Inca culture. We in fact helped to create the "cuts" in the stone and directed others how to move through the dimensions of time. The small stone that your teacher gave you is a connection to the space/time energy.

> Call on us to help you learn to move into the past, present, and future. Continue to experiment so you can more easily move beyond this three-dimensional plane of experience. We have come into your life at this time to teach you how to travel outside of time, as you now know it. Practice, open yourself to this possibility, and ask for our help and guidance.

We have given you our individual names but names are really unimportant. We will use them, but we simply are named the Three. We have grown together over thousands of your years. In reality we are not separate. By calling ourselves the Three, we give you a clue about time. We each embody a dimensionality that is far beyond what you know as past, present, and future. There is no time except in the dream that you call your reality. At some point you too will know what is beyond time and space, but learning to move outside of time and holding everything as only one thing, you will have to deeply experience what you call full awakening. You will experience that there is a vastness where everything is present and all actions occur simultaneously. These are just words but they are words to help you experience reality directly.

Second Comment

Among other teachings, the three parts to *Energy Teachings of the Three*: The Five Pillars of Love, The Five Foundation Stones for Daily Living, and The Challenges for the End Times, were given to me over the span of six years. The Three emphasized that the practices given in each section need to be practiced daily to bring about a transformation of healing and Love in one's life.

- The practices of the Five Pillars of Love focus on opening and increasing the energy frequencies of our heart-mind in order to transform the way we experience the power of Love in our daily lives.
- The Five Foundation Stones for Daily Living are psycho-spiritual practices to release the threads that make up the tapestry or structure of our ego-identity so that we can discover the truth of our life.
- The practices of the Challenges of the End Times is how to prepare to face the fears and uncertainties of our life as the earth and our world civilization begin to collapse. These practices teach us how to live with others in the context of community in order to survive and thrive.

I have found that both the information and the practices in this material have been challenging, inspiring, and deeply provocative in my life. I am deeply grateful for these teachings and believe that as you contemplate the information and take on the practices you will experience a profound experience of the presence of the Three with you.

In one communication, the Three told me that in the vastness of the universe there is only "one thing" occurring. Therefore, they said, "You and we are one being. We are all bundles of energy taking on forms to learn and grow. Remember, there is only one energy and that is Love."

> **You and we are one being. We are all bundles of energy taking on forms to learn and grow. Remember, there is only one energy and that is Love.**

The Five Pillars of Love

*T*he Five Pillars of Love explore the energies, frequencies, and the foundations of Love in our lives. First we will provide some context about the energy of Love. We have said before that Love is the force that is the fundamental *binder* of the Universe. Love is a universal force that all beings experience directly because Love is the fundamental building block of all life and all existence.

> **Love is a force that is the fundamental *binder*
> of the Universe.**

We know from our experience and explorations that the Singularity that brought manifestation into form is this Love. We could call it a creator god, a principle, a primary force or All That Is. However, neither the terms Love as the Principal Force nor All That Is fully express its true nature. We can also describe Love as essence, consciousness, and the Manifold. But words and concepts can never describe the reality and direct knowing of the nature of Love.

Remember, Love is not an emotion or a feeling. Rather, it is better described as attraction, connection, merging, knowing, and presence. We obviously can go on and on and describe Love in many different ways as to what it is and what it is not. The poets and mystics of your world have attempted to find the words and the beauty to describe the inherent nature of Love. In very simple terms, *we would describe Love as the fundamental energy that is everything. We say energy because energy represents fundamental movement, action, and creation.* We provide this discussion as a context for the difficulty to describe Love itself. Let us now turn to some of its energetic components, which you might call, "The Five Pillars of Love."

With regard to the phrase, "The Five Pillars of Love," we used the word *Pillars* as it represents the five aspects on which Love rests. These are five frequencies of energies as we've expressed them. This phrase will be best for some people and another phrase that is similar—"The Five Frequencies of Love"—will be appropriate for others. Simply understand that these five are the practical and energetic foundations for experiencing and practicing Love in one's life.

> **Remember, Love is not an emotion or a feeling. Rather, it is better described as attraction, connection, merging, knowing, and presence.**

These five pillars are the energetic forces that open and connect you to the power, expression, creation, and manifestation of the direct knowing and experience of the nature of Love within you and within all beings. These five energy forms with their practices are what every spiritual tradition teaches. What we present to you is the means to awaken your energy matrix that has been covered over by the warp and weft of a mind structure, which has isolated and cut you off from your true nature. Although we present a context of information and insights to you, the important aspect of each pillar and energy teaching is in the practices. Your willingness and commitment to practice these energy forms is what will move you into the fifth dimension of light that is Love.

Our purpose in providing this information and these practices is to assist whoever is drawn to this material to be guided in the process of releasing the woven tapestry of their thoughts, memories, and emotions that binds them to a reality system that covers the truth of existence as it actually is. The practices that form the *Energy Teachings of the Three* will be useful to people in different ways and in different stages of their life and their personal and spiritual development. Any one practice done with commitment, intention, and consistency will open the doorway of Love and lead the person home to a dimension of reality that is beyond their current perception.

> **What we present to you is the means to awaken your energy matrix that has been covered by the warp and weft of a mind structure, which has isolated and cut you off from your true nature.**

Let us begin now with the Five Pillars of Love, the first one being Appreciation.

Appreciation

Pillar One

Appreciation as a component energy of Love is connected to the perception of reality. *Appreciation changes the focal length of perception.*

To appreciate is to *see* what is truly present for you. Appreciation connects you to the other. Appreciation perceives a person, animal, tree, sunset, or whatever else one confronts you in life with a different quality of seeing. Appreciation is seeing more deeply into that person or thing.

First of all, *appreciation changes and charges the field of your own energy pattern.* **This shift connects you directly to universal Love**. The more you choose to see the good and the beautiful, and be conscious of looking at the essence of what that person or situation or encounter truly is, then the more you create a larger field of energy, light, and connection. This field of energy bridges and creates an enfolding field between you and the other that "strikes a bell" of a positive energy charge that changes both your energy field and the other person's.

> To appreciate is to see what is truly present for you. Appreciation connects you directly to universal Love.

Let us present some of the impacts of that charged field:

1. That energy moment of mutual appreciation generates a field that opens you and the other to a higher frequency filled with greater awareness.
2. In that field is the potential to shift the focal point of reality to perceive in new and startling ways.
3. In that moment you and the other transcend individual ego states, personality differences, and your mutual self-centeredness.
4. You feel and know that you are at a different level of consciousness in that moment.
5. The energy charge of appreciation activates the feeling state between you and the other by shifting mood, attitude, and consciousness as well as by releasing unconscious beliefs.
6. In that moment of appreciation, you perceive directly without judgment or preconception.
7. In that moment you access an energy that lets you penetrate through to the essence of reality clearly and directly.

At a practical level, appreciation focuses on qualities, characteristics, capabilities, and capacities. Appreciation is an act of perceiving deeply what people can do, how something looks, and how some quality is expressed by a person or thing. You can be grateful for it, but basically appreciation is other-centered in perception. It is seeing into the other what is actually present, unique, expressive, and expansive. But you can as well be appreciative of qualities, characteristics, capabilities, and so on in yourself. Gratitude comes from having experienced self-appreciation and all that it creates in you. Self-appreciation is simply another means to have Love for yourself.

Judgment is what stops your appreciation and penetration of seeing others, the world, and yourself more deeply. When you judge people, animals, trees, situations, or anything, you close down that focal length of perception. You no longer see and feel what is true in the world. The focal length of your seeing becomes short, drawn back close to you, and your potential new perception is broken up by your beliefs, judgments, fears, and conditioning.

> **Judgment is what stops your appreciation and penetration of seeing others, the world, and yourself more deeply.**

Practice

Practicing appreciation daily releases this close-in perception of self-protection with its pseudo reality that limits your joy, your freedom, and your lightness of being.

Every day, look for people and situations about which to express your appreciation. This practice is simply to see who or what they are or what they are doing, and acknowledge what you see. For example, you see a cat stretched out on a windowsill and you say, "You look beautiful in your relaxation." Or, you are at work and observe someone working late and you speak your appreciation to the effort they are making. You hear a beautiful piece of music with a string solo and pause to appreciate the talent of the person playing the violin.

Here are some further suggestions for you:

1. As you see an element in a person or situation to appreciate, speak it out loud, don't just think it.
2. Tell the person or thing what it is you are appreciating.
3. As you speak it, feel the energy of the speaking coming from your heart. Touch your heart as you speak.
4. As you connect with the other from this heart speaking, you will feel a charge of energy build between you and the other.

If appropriate, acknowledge and tell the person about the energy sensation you feel toward them.

5. If you find you are focused on judging someone or something, shift your focus and look for something you can appreciate in the person or situation you are judging.

6. Even if there is not a strong energy feeling when you speak your appreciation, a shift of energy will begin in you.

7. *By interrupting the cycle of judging with appreciation, you generate a strong awareness to build and expand your energy rather than contract it.*

8. Keep the appreciation going throughout the day. The more you appreciate consistently throughout the day the more the energy will build in you and the greater will become the clarity of your perception.

9. Practice this for two or three weeks consistently and you will find that your perception has changed. You are grounding this Pillar of Love in your life as a natural part of who you are.

Meditate on this practice and more will become apparent for you. Know that we Three deeply appreciate you. Feel our appreciation coming to you. Take it into your body-mind-heart right now from us. There is no space or time from when we originally speak these words. There is only the now, the present as you read this. When one appreciates another, as we are doing to you, new energy emerges in the one being appreciated. This is true not only for humans, but for animals, trees, sunsets, music—everything—for all things are conscious.

Be blessed in Appreciation.

Compassion

Pillar Two

So, now we turn to the Pillar of Love called compassion.

Just as appreciation changes the focal length of perception, **compassion opens awareness at the level of understanding.** To understand is to be in the place where you have the direct and same experience as the other.

When you break down the word *compassion* you have *com* meaning "with" and *passion* as "that which drives one's energy and motivation." *Through compassion, one lets go of self-perception and aligns into and combines with the movement, drive, energy, and experience of the other*. In this sense, compassion is not a feeling or an emotion. Compassion is becoming unified with the energetic field of the other.

In compassion, one attunes to the frequency of the other. So, when you say you feel compassion for another, what you *feel* is the core essence of their energy condition. This is a state in which you do not have sympathy, concern, or caring for that person. *Sympathy, concern*, and *caring* are words that create separation from the other. You will have energy *feelings*, but the feelings are matching the energy feeling of the other. The difference is that as you respond in compassion to another you will hold an awareness of a larger context for the energy condition of the other person.

As you, together with the other, align with the higher frequency, you both can transform the quality and state condition of each other's experience.

Simply, to have compassion for another—person, animal, country, tree, weather, and so on—is to hold a context in which the higher frequency energy of Love "stands under" and holds both of you. It is being with the other in the same frequency while holding for both of you the larger frequency of what is the essence of reality—that is of Love—without separation, judgment, or a sense of fundamental difference between you and the other.

> **Simply, to have compassion for another—person, animal, country, tree, weather, and so on—is to hold a context in which the higher frequency energy of Love "stands under" and holds both of you.**

Being in the same *higher* energy frequency with the other is to stand together with their true nature *and* in your own true nature.

When being together in the one True Nature, both of you are experiencing an aligned frequency that is higher, larger, and stronger than any condition, circumstance, or environment that both of you are facing in a particular time and space.

Your Dalai Lama, who is considered the embodiment of compassion, holds for his people a higher frequency that permits him to hold the pain, suffering, and destructiveness of Tibet without separating himself from the Chinese. He has understanding and experience of the frequency of the Chinese, just as he does for his own people. His role in exhibiting compassion is not just to hold the frequency of pain and suffering, but rather to be in a higher-level frequency for both the Tibetan people and the Chinese people at the same time.

The practice of compassion is the queen of the five pillars of Love. It is the transformation of the deep mother quality that respects and understands all of her children and does not hold back from her caring and actions to redeem, save, and protect all beings, with her frequency of the supreme energy of Love.

> **To deepen your compassion is to increasingly shift your perceptual understanding about your own pain and suffering.**

Practice

To deepen your compassion is to increasingly shift your perceptual understanding of your own pain and suffering. For your compassion to grow, you need to know that you are connected to the source of All That Is, who is holding, protecting, and caring for you!

Step One

1. The first practice is to acknowledge the frequency, the energetic feeling, of your own pain and suffering.
2. *Literally name the suffering and pain, understand it, and then shift your awareness and focus to the frequency of your heart, and bring the specific issues and experiences that create your pain and suffering to that heart place.*
3. As you hold these conditions at your heart, feel a warming, a pulsing, an electrical feeling, or any other sensation of energy increase, then move this heart energy to the crown of your head. Feel the sensation of energy building in you, in the same way you did at the heart.
4. Then let this energy go out the top of your head and experience the expansion of your being, of the Love that you truly are.

5. *In this expanded space let yourself see, feel, and experience your pain and suffering dissolving in this greater frequency of expansion.*
6. You may have to do this practice again and again as new issues of pain and suffering emerge from your awareness.
7. What you will notice as you practice self-compassion is that you will naturally become attuned to this higher vibration and frequency of Love most of the time.

Step Two

After you've worked with your own self-compassion, turn your attention toward other people and beings in your life.

1. With another person, the practice is to first connect to the highest frequency you know from the expanded frequency you've practiced for yourself, and reach out mentally and with your feelings from your heart-mind to the other.
2. Let that frequency connect with and understand—stand with—the frequency of the other.
3. As you practice this compassionate frequency extending to another, it will be similar to how you've been working with your own self-compassion. Extending toward another in this way, you will find that it is easier to connect to their frequency than you realize. *It is moving out of focus on yourself to focusing on matching your frequency with that of the other and then expanding to that larger, higher, and more expansive frequency that encompasses you both.* This is when you will experience a true and deep connection of Love with another that holds no judgment of what they or you are experiencing.
4. You see and know in the other what you've seen and known in yourself. And you know that, whatever is the pain and suffering of another, it can be healed in them.

5. Start practicing with animals, trees, family, and friends close to you.
6. All you have to do is inwardly ask if you can connect with them. Simply extending to them is to understand from their point of reference. This shifts you and their frequency, and opens the connection of understanding as to who and what they are experiencing.
7. You then expand together to a higher frequency that brings caring, comfort, and a sense of their true nature as a being.
8. If something concretely and practically needs to be done for that other person as part of the act of compassion, it will not be done with condescension but with an equality of mutual Love. **This is called Love in action.**

> **Compassion is not a feeling or an emotion. Compassion is becoming unified with the energetic field of the other.**

Be blessed in your connection, understanding, and compassion for all beings.

Forgiveness

Pillar Three

Now we move to the next Pillar of Love. We turn to that energetic aspect of Love called forgiveness.

Forgiveness is a powerful characteristic of healing and transformation for the individual and for use in many group situations. Its power and energy and healing lie in its use by an individual.

Just as appreciation is about perception (seeing) and compassion gives a place to understanding, *forgiveness is an energy of release*.

Your ego weaves a pattern of energetic containment within and around you. This pattern of containment binds thoughts, experiences, attitudes, behaviors, and most of all, emotional projections both from you to yourself and to you from others. The weaving pattern of this heart-mind becomes distorted by how these projections become fixated in the energetic structure of the body, in one's emotions, and in the mind. It is this woven structure that we call, or rather you call, the ego identity. You are nothing more nor less than this woven pattern of inner and outer projections. In truth they have no reality, but you and all humans live and act as though you are real.

> **Your ego weaves a pattern of energetic containment within and around you. This pattern of containment binds thoughts, experiences, attitudes, behaviors, and most of all, emotional projections both from you to yourself and to you from others.**
>
> **You are nothing more nor less than this woven pattern of inner and outer projections.**

Forgiveness is the energy that releases the binding structure of the projections that have been woven into your ego identity that you call yourself. All your shame, guilt, terror, anger, and fear are the tapestry of your daily experience of existence.

The manner in which forgiveness releases the bindings of projections is to release the energy within the binding process itself. The projections either from you or to you are forms of energy that naturally dissipate if they are not held bound to the mind-heart. **It is the drive to hold onto these projections that keep weaving together your unique tapestry you call your identity.**

If you begin to release these projections—by literally letting the energy of these projections dissipate and move back into the vast energy flux of existence—your ego structure begins to dissolve and evaporate. This is what happens at the death of the body. The mind-heart is attempting to dissolve all of the projections and unravel the tapestry of the woven ego identity that has been created over a lifetime.

Now, what is important to understand is that forgiveness is simply another type of projection that can penetrate the ego-tapestry of woven projections. *Forgiveness is a projection. It is a thought or energy form with a higher frequency of energy that acts like a laser beam that melts and dissolves the binding projections of shame, guilt, fear, anger, and all inner negativity.*

It is important to remember that your negative projections toward others (in the form of judgments, self-justifications, and special-ness—the view of being superior—as well as outright anger, resentment, hurt, and abuse of others) are all woven into your identity tapestry. Both one's own "hurts" and the "hurting" of others are the energetic projections that forgiveness can dissolve.

For an energy projection to dissolve both the positive and negative projections of your identity, you have to reformulate a different relationship to your heart-mind. We use the term heart-mind because, as the Buddhists and others in your traditions use it, this term suggests that the energy of forgiveness comes from a practice that releases a combined energy from feeling and thought— the heart and mind.

All negative projections come from feelings and thoughts. For example, feelings and thoughts come into being by the expression of your anger and judgments or by your shame and rationalizations.

Forgiveness, however, raises the frequency of feeling and thought to a much higher frequency. Through that process, forgiveness becomes laser-like in its ability to project into a situation of feeling and thought. This higher frequency energy—laser-like—is not as complicated as it may appear to be to you. The simple act of projecting forgiveness teaches you its power and its gift.

What binds a higher frequency of feeling and thought together is intention. Notice we say feeling rather than emotion. Emotions are the results of and responses to positive and negative feeling projections. The more you "flood" projections, for example, with the continuing emotions of self-pity, longing, and self-justification, the more you bind and fixate the feeling projections into your ego identity of victimhood. One can project the opposite as victor, superior being, as an all-knowing or even enlightened person, which also binds and fixates one's feeling and identity. It is the same with thoughts. As you focus on one thought pattern continually, that thought pattern is woven into the tapestry of your identity. *It is thought that fixates beliefs and actions into a pattern and rationale for your "normal" behavior.*

> **All negative projections come from feeling and thought. Forgiveness, however, raises the frequency of feeling and thought to a much higher frequency.**

Practice

So, the practice of forgiveness is relatively simple. There are many techniques and methods that people suggest as the means for activating the higher frequency of the feeling-thought energy of forgiveness. The focus of this practice is to dissolve the deeply held projections that bind your ego identity together so as to release you into a state of freedom.

1. First you are to hold at the heart of this forgiveness process an intention to focus the feeling-thought on acceptance and release of whatever fear, depression, pain, rejection, hurt, shame, anger, action, reaction, and/or failure you have for yourself or for others. The intention of this acceptance and release is held in a state of deep relaxation in your body.

2. Take time to breathe into your body parts, asking your body to accept, relax, open, and release. Relaxation is the beginning of forgiveness as a higher frequency projection that naturally dissolves your feeling-thought patterns by penetrating your ego identity.

3. As relaxation deepens, light energy naturally comes forth within you and you may feel this energy as a tingling sensation

moving in your hands and in other parts of your body. The sensations can also occur as heat beginning to arise throughout your body or simply as a calm and restfulness settling upon you. Whichever way you sense the light, you will know it as a lifting up of your body, thoughts, and feelings to a deeper place of *knowing* within you. As you breathe and relax, attune to this emerging light. Bring this light to your heart. Feel its warming, pulsating, and tingling sensation. Let your heart be nurtured by this healing light.

4. As you feel the warmth and relaxation, be aware of the light sensations moving from your heart center up through your body and then moving up and out of the top of your head.

5. Focus on your crown chakra at the top of the head. The heart-mind energy naturally merges with a higher frequency light energy that is always present and waiting for this pathway connection. This emergence of higher frequency energy begins a releasing of the projection bindings that hold your identity ego pattern together.

6. With this merging of energy, let this light energy expand out from around you. As the dissolving occurs, your thoughts and feelings will quiet and an awareness of peace, tranquility, and a deepening awareness will arise. As you rest in this awareness observe the difference in your feeling-thought state.

7. You do not know what specifically to forgive consciously because when you move into this clear heart-mind or feeling-thought projection of forgiveness, Love energy is doing the work. Trust that this high frequency energy will dissolve what is needed at that moment of time.

8. In essence, as you work intentionally with forgiveness in this way, you are dissolving the tapestry of your woven ego identity.

We would give a caution. Those who enter this high frequency state can, with their intention, blast the ego tapestry too strongly. This "blasting" can shatter the ego too quickly and a person can feel overwhelmed and lost. However, if one stays with the light energy in their heart, this overwhelmed and lost sensation will find a great release and freedom and a rebalancing of their heart-mind. Remember, you must trust that as you attune to this heart-mind energy frequency of forgiveness you will dissolve the tapestry of your ego projections in the manner that is in your own rhythm and timing. This will permit your natural awakening. So, be gentle and loving to yourself, but know that the energy source is guiding you.

Let us provide you with a summary of these steps:

1. Focus on your intention of releasing projections.
2. Breathe relaxation, acceptance, and openness into your body.
3. As you breathe, attune to the energy and light arising within you.
4. Be aware of light moving from your heart up out of the top of your head.
5. At the top of your head, light merges with higher frequency energy. This dissolves your projections.
6. Let this merging expand out from you as much as you can.
7. Notice peace deepen in you as light energy expands around you.
8. Trust that Love energy (this is forgiveness) is naturally dissolving particular aspects of your woven tapestry of projections.

May you know and experience the full dissolving of your ego tapestry in the manner and timing that brings you to full forgiveness and awakening.

Kindness

Pillar Four

In general society, Kindness is a practice of being considerate and temperate with yourself and others. Kindness is to perceive and care for the needs of yourself as well as the needs of others. Kindness is an attitude of acceptance that holds that whatever the circumstance or condition, you respond without judgment or a stance of superiority.

These are the common characteristics you would apply to kindness. However, at the energetic level, kindness as an aspect of Love *is an energy that opens the quality of insight.* When you experience or see the energy of kindness from one person to another, there is a spark of recognition that there is no difference between you and the other. The same thing happens when someone offers you kindness—you recognize there is no difference between the two of you.

> **At the energetic level, kindness as an aspect of Love is an energy that opens the quality of insight.**

To be kind is to open your energy field to perceive needs or to simply extend to another for the sake of goodwill and caring.

Kindness is an energy that is always noticing, looking for ways to act in order that the heart energy can expand more and mutually connect with all beings in the world of existence.

Being kind to yourself, to other humans, animals, plants, trees, birds, and more, as well as to made objects such as tools, cars, homes, and so on increases the energetic connection within the web of existence. Kindness moves you into heart connection and weaves into you the mystery of unity.

So, the energy of kindness is the key for continuing to expand and open that energy, which is your foundation to experience true reality.

Your Dalai Lama says that his religion is kindness. He knows from inner knowledge that kindness is the outer action that shifts patterns and opens new awareness. It is kindness that takes you to the heart of Love's power, healing, knowledge, creativity, and revelation.

The energy of kindness is transforming not only for you by expressing it, but also for those receiving it.

Kindness generates energy and creates a higher vibration frequency. This frequency moves quickly toward the spectrum of light. In kindness, things lighten up!

There is a gentleness that is part of kindness. Kindness cannot truly be driven by ego. There are so many stories in all your religious and spiritual traditions of your civilization about the true nature of kindness. The story of the wealthy man who proclaims to the world the great amount he is giving to the impoverished contrasts with the story of the old woman who shares out of Love what little food she has to the starving children of her neighborhood. These stories reflect that *kindness isn't about actions, but about intent.* The action of kindness is not about what is done, but rather the heart frequency that motivates the action.

This action of true kindness is initiated from insight. "Oh, I see. That is what is needed here. I see that that's what I could do in this moment for the other."

The action of kindness is not about what is done, but rather the heart frequency that motivates the action.

Practice

All around you are opportunities to express kindness. *True kindness requires a deeper energetic perceiving. Kindness gains insight naturally as you attune to a frequency of the forehead and crown chakras.*

In meditation, whether walking or just sitting quietly, *focus your attention on the forehead and the crown chakras simultaneously. Hold your attention until you feel warmth, buzzing, pulsation, or whatever sensation begins to shift your awareness.* Move this energy of awareness down into your heart and feel its expansion within you. Hold the awareness that this expanding heart energy is kindness to yourself.

1. After meditation practice, attempt to hold your dual awareness of these two points simultaneously (forehead and crown) as you move through your day.
2. At first, you will need to be conscious of these points. In time they will be your natural radar for expressing kindness. You will begin to see people and situations in new ways and provide appropriate actions of kindness.
3. When this new seeing opens in you, be gentle and patient with yourself. Notice what would be appropriate to do in the moment or at some ideal time.
4. *Bring that energy of seeing down into your heart and ask if you are to do or not do some outward action in response to what you*

see. If you are to act, ask, *"What is it that is to be done here, not by me, but by the energy of Love flowing through me."*

5. With awareness and practice you will see into a situation and know what the appropriate action will be. You will know because, being attuned to the forehead and crown and bringing that energy into your heart, you will channel the energy of Love into the kindness act.

6. The more you hold these two points and bring them to the heart, the more naturally you will live in an aura of kindness for yourself and other beings.

7. To see into a person, animal, situation, or object is to see what and how is the appropriate response.

8. Kindness is always appropriate to the insight, to the seeing within at the center of what the kindness can serve.

> **Kindness gains insight naturally as you attune to a frequency of the forehead and crown chakras.**

Practice, then, this frequency of kindness. It will bring caring and goodness to yourself and all beings you touch.

Gratitude

Pillar Five

Now for the energy and pillar of Gratitude!

Gratitude we save for last, as it is what Love floats on. We use the word *floats* because the energy of gratitude is a resting place for Love in your heart. It floats there because gratitude is fluid and moves quickly to any person or situation rapidly and easily.

Gratitude is all encompassing. Gratitude shapes your life to be in rhythm and harmony with all of life's experiences. What gratitude does is lighten every person and event you encounter. With gratitude, patience naturally is present. Gratitude reveals the gifts in everything. Joy, happiness, and peace are the natural and basic experiences when you look at life through the lens of gratitude.

The energy of gratitude is at a very slow frequency. Gratitude slows you down to see, feel, and experience depth, clarity, and understanding of any person, event, or experience. What may seem to be negative when viewed through the lens of gratitude is seen as a teaching, a gift, and a means for emerging from the illusion of existence.

Gratitude opens you to experience reality as it actually is, not as it may appear to be. In this respect gratitude is *magic*.

Gratitude penetrates illusion and shatters it because the only thing that is real is the Love that holds everything together—both the positive and negative, the dark and the light, the male and the female, the earth and the sky. Love literally holds all the opposites of this illusionary force. When you live in a constant state of gratitude you are fully awake to the light of who you truly are and there are no opposites.

Gratitude is the jewel that every being at all levels of existence comes to finally experience as the entrance to all worlds, all dimensions, and all realms of existence and being. It is a lesson we Three at our level continue to learn and deepen within the realm we are experiencing. We know gratitude is the doorway to the heart of Love's existence.

> Gratitude we save for last, as it is what Love floats on. We use the word *floats*, because the energy of gratitude is a resting place for Love in your heart. It floats there because gratitude is fluid and moves quickly to any person or situation rapidly and easily.

Practice

Here is a simple practice that keeps gratitude at the forefront of awareness in your life.

1. First, make a list of all the things you are grateful for and a list of all the things you are not grateful for. Doing this ungrateful list at first sharpens your consciousness of what you resist in being grateful and those daily experiences for which you don't feel gratitude. Keep adding to your list for several days both the positive and negative gratitude statements. As you list the

big and small experiences you will be surprised at what you perceive.

2. This part of the practice begins to slow down your awareness and sharpens your observation and insight.

3. At the same time as you are making the two lists, whether you observe positive gratitude or what you are not grateful for, simply say to yourself, *Thank you* to both. *Be neutral to both.* After a few days of saying "Thank you," add to the "Thank you" with an awareness of your heart. Simply, when you say, "Thank you," touch your heart area in the middle of your chest.

4. After a few more days of saying "Thank you" and touching your heart, add a warm feeling of energy vibration as you speak your thanks and touch your heart. *The words, the physical touch, and the feeling will begin to open the Love doorway wider and wider for you.*

5. After some days of practice, you will literally see and feel the light in both the positive and the negative experiences you list.

Let us repeat the sequence again:

1. Make two lists, one of positive things for which to be grateful, the other of negative things for which to be ungrateful; keep adding to the lists.

2. For a few days, say the words "Thank you" for both the positive and negative people, situations, and events you experience.

3. A few days later, touch your heart area when you say, "Thank you" for both positive and negative events.

4. After a few more days of saying the words, "Thank you" and touching your heart area, feel a warm sensation at the heart as you touch it and say the words.

5. Keep this practice going until you begin to feel and see the light in all things through this lens of gratitude.

> **When you live in a constant state of gratitude, you are fully awake to the light of who you truly are and there are no opposites. We know gratitude is the doorway to the heart of Love's existence.**

Let us now provide some other practices for developing gratitude as a natural function of your life. These practices will help to open the gratitude gate within you.

1. Make a list of all the things, people, events, situations, and experiences in your life that have supported, inspired, and motivated you over the past three to five years. As you write and review the list, feel in your heart center gratitude for each one of them.
2. When you take a walk, name and acknowledge the trees, clouds, animals, flowers, people, and so on that you see. As you name them, feel the gratitude in your heart as you place a hand to your heart area. Thank each entity for their existence and for being present for you. Remember, everything is alive and conscious. Everything is animated with being and awareness.
3. At every meal, thank the food and all the people and beings who are nourishing your body to stay alive.
4. Make a list of the key positive people and key negative people in your life. Thank both for being your teachers.
5. List key family and friends, and everyday feel gratitude that they are part of your life.
6. Give thanks daily as you see expressions of the four elements of nature and the spirits that embody them:
    - Water: rain, faucet water, pond, stream, river, lake, ocean
    - Earth: rock, dirt, the land you walk on, mountains, desert, jungle
    - Fire: flames, wood burning, the sun, candles
    - Air: the wind, breeze, smells, the breath in your lungs

Finally, let us say to you that the nature of gratitude is more than a concept. It is one of the universal principles that begins and extends the growth of awareness in a person. It is what opens a person toward full realization. *If there is only one practice that you do, giving gratitude for everything would be the doorway to awakening.*

> Say aloud, "I am thankful for my life. I am grateful that I can see or experience this right now."

Your Saint Francis of Assisi made everything in his life a prayer of gratitude. Birds, animals, flowers, insects, children—all were drawn toward him because they felt his clear seeing of them through the lens of gratitude. You, too, please take on the practice of gratitude as much as you can in order to discover its true power and transformation in your own life.

Every time you start to judge or criticize or feel you are separating yourself from others, from trees, animals, or anything, stop your mind and be grateful for it. Simply say to yourself or even better say aloud, *"I am thankful for my life. I am grateful that I can see or experience this right now."* Any statement like this that acknowledges your gratitude will shift your perception and then your feeling state. This is how gratitude works to transform your life.

We hope this gives you another piece of the gratitude practice.

How Does Gratitude Transform Reality?

First consider the nature of Gratitude itself. Gratitude is an energy that alters how one perceives the world. Consider the opposite of gratitude, which is a basic disregard and thanklessness of what has been given to you, expressed for you, or received by you in your life. When you have no gratitude, you contract your senses, feelings, and perception into a narrow self-centered focus. The flow and magic of existence shuts down for you. On the other hand, with gratitude, your awareness, perception, and body sensation expands. *Gratitude increases the vibration and energy of the heart center and increases the pulsation of the nervous system as neurons fire off in new patterns that generate joy, happiness, freedom, and inner contentment.*

Gratitude catalyzes the field of energy in a person by radiating a higher frequency of light photons within the body. The greater the heart gratitude in you, the greater your mind becomes illuminated. The useless mind chatter dies away and clarity of perception opens. The more you focus on gratitude, the more you surrender the conditioned mind with its narrow band of focus. Awareness expands as gratitude increases within you. Naturally there is a new energy vitality and coherence between the mind and the heart. The natural result of that heart-mind coherence is joy, gentleness, consideration, and deep caring for yourself and others.

It is because of this heart-mind coherence that gratitude is a transformation of reality for you. Among forgiveness, appreciation, kindness, and compassion, **gratitude is the key transformer of reality perception.** Everything that you feel, see, and understand becomes transformed into beauty, clarity, and a more holistic and integrated reality, which continues to grow and expand into every area of your life.

We hope this short explanation gives you some understanding of this intuitive knowledge you have for the power of gratitude. You can feel how it raises the vibration of your heart. Continue to deepen your practice of gratitude throughout all aspects of your life.

May the peace, the joy, and the wisdom of gratitude continue to transform you.

> When you live in a constant state of gratitude, you are fully awake to the light of who you truly are and there are no opposites. We know gratitude is the doorway to the heart of Love's existence.

Implications of the Five Pillars Practices

*T*hese five pillars for Love's presence in your life will become your foundation and generate and establish a new frequency of evolving so that Love becomes your reality.

Practice and continue to be in this feeling state, this heart state of gratitude. Remember that everything in your life is a form of blessing and increases the deep awareness of your connection to this vast principle of Love. *Remember, we describe Love as the universal principle that generates all forms of energy, light, awareness, and consciousness.*

Love is the highest frequency of creativity. Love is the foundation for all aspects of true reality. Reality is not physical. It is the multi-dimensional experience of one thing always occurring. You call this one thing light, energy, God, the singularity, the manifold expression of everything.

> **Reality is not physical. It is the multi-dimensional experience of one thing always occurring.**

Your scientists, who explore the edge of this vastness, touch this experience and feel and know at some level of their being that Love is what they are. Their minds, their hearts, their very beings are flooded not only with knowledge, but with an infinite knowing and awareness. When they do their mathematics, they touch a language that is free of pejorative and subjective experience. The symbols of mathematics introduce one into the mechanics and the universal understanding of the next layer of reality beyond your so-called physical reality. In your current evolutionary development as a civilization, mathematics has taken you through an industrial and technological pattern that is ultimately destructive to the human species, all non-human species, and the planet itself. The principles of Love were not strongly present to ground this knowledge.

This planet has seen several cycles at mental and spiritual development. Each cycle has taught the species certain things and brought the evolution of humans to a different level of civilization.

Our Lemurian civilization was destroyed because power and energy were corrupted by beings who had developed both physical and psychic abilities. The ego development, as you would call it today, was distorted by a belief that they knew the laws and principles of inter-dimensional travel and were using them for power and dominance over others. That civilization was at the threshold of transformation and could have become a member of a vast expression of interconnection and movement toward discovering the transformation of time and space. Because the principles of Love were not strong enough, that civilization destroyed itself.

In the same way as before, there are individuals in your civilization who are shifting and transforming, and learning to move out of time and space. These are and were the same individuals who were in our civilization when it experienced that shift. They are again at a crossroads. Will they find the balance in the principles and reality of Love? We Three represent many who discovered these mathematical and energy *laws*, but we also discovered and practiced the energies of Love. We do not judge these other individuals. It takes many seeds before a few plants flower. Love sows the seeds again and again, and the principles and practices of Love bring the flowering.

There are many at this time who have this potential to flower. There are many others who are at the cusp, the threshold of transformation. You all have evolved through many lifetimes in order to come to this life. You are now present for the possibility of transformation both for yourselves and also to assist many others. Now at the end of your time on this planet, the pressure is mounting for transformation—a transformation that at this stage is beyond your comprehension.

Every transformation requires a high intensity of energy. It needs both positive and negative polarities. It is obvious to everyone that this tension is happening worldwide. So, you have fear and Love as the polarities. We have given you the principles and energetic practices of the Five Pillars of Love to help you and others increase the tension through the frequency of Love. On the negative polarity, many other forces are growing the fear through hatred, pain, suffering, control, and misinformation. These are the five pillars of fear. What the five Pillars of Love provide is a pathway to increase the positive tension and heal these five pillars of fear.

> On the negative polarity, many other forces are growing the fear through hatred, pain, suffering, control, and misinformation. *These are the five pillars of fear.*
>
> The Five Pillars of Love provide a pathway to increase the positive tension and heal these five pillars of fear.

You are in a vast mystery with a complexity that no one person or group can control or even understand. **It is not faith, but courage that moves your frequency daily into the five pillars of Love**. Share the practices so many more individuals can begin to understand that Love is a force that breaks up confusion, uncertainty, despair, and slavery to one's ego identity. When the tapestry that has been woven into your separation from the higher frequencies of Love has been dissolved, then something beyond your imagining or experience emerges in you. This other "something" is a different dimension of being—it is a being in a frequency that we call *light*. However, it is not light as you know it in your dimension. The energy system of your body-mind is designed to move toward this higher frequency of light. As you become this light energy, there is no longer the experience of living in time and space. You who are at the cusp of this light now will cross over, and you will be transformed into another dimension.

Crossing the Threshold: Practicing the Five Pillars of Love

The core teachings about the Five Pillars of Love are what we want to give to you at this moment in your life and that of your civilization. Remember, they are essentially practices that retool your energy system. It is up to you and the others with whom you share these five pillars to commit and engage in the practices daily. You've tried each one a little bit as they were presented to you, but now be systematic and learn to experience what these frequency practices can create in you. *Most important is to dissolve the tapestry of your ego structure. The five pillars help you release this tapestry.*

Once again, your ego tapestry is a continual weaving together of your projections about yourself, others, and the world around you. You don't see reality as it actually is because the tapestry of projections you've woven and the projections of others toward you create a cocoon of self-illusion. You believe that these self and other projections are real and substantive.

What are these projections? They are the beliefs, experiences, and environments—family, friends, school, work, media—that you've interpreted as real for you. They are glued together by pain, confusion, shame, longing, doubt, and uncertainty, among other negative expressions. **These negative projections reduce direct perception of existence to self-projections that reinforce one's sense of beliefs and identity.** There are also positive experiences of "imaginary" friends, friendly animals, nurturing by parents, and exploring with playmates. You have experienced that the environment around you as you grew as a child was both threatening and magical. You feared and you had wonder. It was both positive and negative.

How positive or negative your experiences have been depends on past karma and current environments and choices made by you and others. Either positive or negative, the projections of self and others determine the level of survival you will feel. *The underlying fear of death or survival in a world where there is little control drives the projections and the interpretation of your experience.* Patterns developed in your life and these created consistency and reliability of how you could move through and survive in the world in the face of your death. As fear grows in you, projections grow. You encase yourself in projected interpretations about people, environments, and yourself. To survive is seen as creating and formulating an ego identity that you present to the world for your survival. **The deep fear you are trying to protect is this little being within you that is both vulnerable and at the same time completely open to reality as it actually is. Others do not see this vulnerable being within you.** These others around you constructed an ego structure to protect themselves from the fear they felt and their own need to survive. And so, they confirmed your fear by projecting their fear onto you.

This is the pattern of consciousness evolution on this planet: pure awareness on first being birthed; then a direct awareness of reality that may last for months or even years; then a blinding by fear through projections on oneself; and the continual development of weaving the tapestry of a self-protective ego identity. However, if you come into this incarnation with a certain amount of energy potential, as well as with karmic potential, this puts you on a journey of reawakening to direct realization. This is a difficult journey for you—it is one of dissolving your identity and releasing yourself from your own and others' projections that have woven your protective cocoon that you call yourself. *This unwinding of all the threads of your ego tapestry is the essential task of this life. At some point, the tapestry will fall away and you will experience freedom.*

Each step of releasing the identity pattern increases the energetic frequency and, at some end point, realization of your true nature as light opens in your consciousness. When this happens, nothing has actually changed in you or around you other than the fact that you now perceive reality directly. This is not magic; rather it is the natural journey that permits you to open to the next step of your evolution. From this next step you now perceive that you are Everything. There is no separation, no fear, and no illusion.

As a human you are flooded with joy, contentment, and openness, and the five pillars of Love have become simply one energy frequency that is existence itself. You look the same, express yourself the same, and though you are moving through time and space, you are not confined by it.

> Appreciation, compassion, forgiveness, kindness, and gratitude are the great gifts of this existence. As you practice each one, you will discover the true secret of reality and the essence of Love.

This is the journey you and so many others have been following all your lives in this incarnation. When you cross the cusp of this threshold we've described, there are no more practices to do; rather there is only living and being what is occurring in each moment. The body changes, emotions come and go, interactions with others happen, the world tumbles through its changes, and you simply magnify some aspect of Love.

Each of the Five Pillars of Love and the other energetic practices we give to you will help you cross the threshold into a different reality. Appreciation, compassion, forgiveness, kindness, and gratitude are the great gifts of this existence. As you practice each one, you will discover the true secret of reality and the essence of Love.

Welcome to your life!

The Five Foundation Stones for Daily Living

We Three have given you the Five Pillars of Love with other energy practices to teach you how to develop your energy patterns at higher level frequencies and to fundamentally transform the nature of your consciousness. The work with these five pillars will help release the woven tapestry of your identity in response to being projected upon by parents, teachers, friends, and institutions, as well as you projecting your reactions outward to create your own self-protective world. Thus, your identity is this illusion and a form of reality that you've woven with your mind. It appears real to you and controls your life and existence until you die. Without learning to achieve a higher level energy frequency you will not be able to break free from this self-created illusion of reality.

All awakening techniques in all traditions rely on changing the energy pattern of the individual. They are for learning to experience energy at a higher frequency and grounding that energy in a new pattern in your life. This is the reason that we have given you the energy teaching grounded in the Five Pillars of Love. Remember, working with these energy exercises is to teach you to awaken to the core essence of existence and your personal existence that is Love. The energy exercises of each pillar focus on opening, clearing, and deepening the heart experience of an individual. As energy exercises, the five pillars are essentially focused on the inward work that you need to do daily to reshape the configuration of your mental, emotional, spiritual, and physical energy patterns.

The Five Foundation Stones for Daily Living provide a complementary function to the Five Pillars of Love. The five foundation stones are Self-Love, Humility, Self-Acceptance, Reflection, and Release of Old Patterns. These five foundational areas are of practical learning for you. We use the image of stones as they represent grounding in the earth and being nourished by an older knowledge and wisdom.

The five daily practices are five foundation stones that give balance to your daily living. These five stones are more psychologically pragmatic and focus on the practices to pull apart the threads of your woven tapestry of identity. *Just as the five pillars work at the energetic level, these five stones work psycho-spiritually. To come to full awakening in a lifetime in the earth configuration, an individual must deal with the dual complementary nature of one's existence. The learning paradigm of earth experience is to release and resolve the fear, shame, self-rejection, self-denial, and self-importance that create your individual false identity. When you release these negative patterns the true essence of what you are naturally opens like a flower. This essence is your Love. Your essence is Love and all that you are is Love. These five stones provide a daily foundation to lead you to your essence.*

These psycho-spiritual stones embody practices to release your woven identity during not only this life but also many other past and future lives. These lives or other forms of existence you've had have taken place not only on this planet but also in many other dimensions. The vastness of your journey and existence is beyond your mental and emotional framework at this time. Recognize that this life is a step on this vast journey.

The energy frequency exercises work on tuning your essence being. However, without focusing on grounding and healing the psychological, mental, and physical aspects of living in this lifetime, you cannot come to the wakening of your True Self. These five stones help you integrate how you've created your perceived and projected world and all the dualities that make up who you've created as a self—material and spiritual, physical and mental-emotional, practical and mystical. Without confronting these dualities directly and working to integrate and heal them, you will carry aspects of your identity forward into the next phase of your journey and will have to continue to work out these issues and dual conditions in other realms. You have the opportunity to transform your identity now in this life. Take advantage of this opportunity now.

> **These stones provide that foundation, practice, and insight to bring this duality into unity within you.**

Each of the five stones lays a foundation for the energy work to rest upon. We started with the energy work because that is what alters the energetic field to actually release the identity pattern that you have created in order to live in this dualistic reality system. The key purpose for learning to live in this dualistic system is not to escape it, but rather to transcend it. Transcend, not in some abstract or mystical way, but rather to live within this duality without being inwardly separated or moving between one dual state and another with an anxiety-disturbed psyche.

As you explore how deep within you is this duality of separation from your essence, from others, and from the true nature of reality as it actually is, you will need grounding, release, and opening to another dimension of yourself. These stones provide that foundation, practice, and insight to bring this duality into unity within you.

All your spiritual teachers attempt to describe how to escape from duality and separation from yourself, God, other beings, and the world itself. *The central learning process of earth experience is to be here and to unify with your True Self and all things in this world.* It is to experience directly what we described in the Five Pillars of Love. It is to experience directly the care, the essence of existence of what you are, which is the core essence of Love. This is Love as the highest form of energy, power, and action that encompasses all of existence. The five pillars of Love provide the leverage points for your discovery of how these frequencies grow and manifest in your life. In the pillars, we gave you the aspects of Love that you have within you and how to experience them more consciously.

These five pillars rest on the foundation stones of daily living. *The work of this earth dimension is to integrate energy with grounding. Together they create transformation.* Together they work to unravel the tapestry that wove together your identity that separated you and isolated you from the reality of this frequency of Love that is your core essence.

Each stone teaches you how to release the threads of your self-created identity. The practices still work with the energy centers as you will experience, but in more pragmatic and grounded ways. The foundation stones and pillars work together and need to be practiced together. We will describe more of how to work with both together, after presenting the five stones.

These five stones—Self-Love, Humility, Self-Acceptance, Reflection, and Release of Old Patterns—work simultaneously with both the inward and outward dimensions of your experience and how you created your life and world in this physical existence. *Each stone reflects the duality of who you really are at essence, and how and what you created that is the opposite of that essence.*

To have self-love and self-acceptance means that you created the opposite, which were shame and self-rejection. Rather than humility, you created the pretense of superiority. Rather than inner and outer reflection you went unconscious and created the mirror of illusion that you were something and someone that you were not. And finally, you built up reinforcing patterns of the past and future that have kept you in a prison where you resisted your freedom, joy, contentment, and peace.

To release your old, self-protective, separating patterns, the five stones help you pull out the key threads of your woven tapestry that hold up the false foundation of your life. Many spiritual and psychological traditions have been taught to work through these same issues. We are giving you a particular lens through which to view these issues, plus a specific language and approach to work with releasing and building a new inner foundation with a new set of psycho-spiritual stones.

These five stones are interconnected and the sequence is significant for you. Use each stone as a building block for your life. Do the practices daily along with the exercises in the Five Pillars of Love. Let us begin to present this material to you.

> To have self-love and self-acceptance means that you created the opposite, which were shame and self-rejection. Rather than humility, you created the pretense of superiority. Rather than inner and outer reflection you went unconscious and created the mirror of illusion that you were something and someone that you were not. And finally, you built up reinforcing patterns of the past and future that have kept you in a prison where you resisted your freedom, joy, contentment, and peace.

Self-Love

Foundation Stone One

Self-love is both a psychological condition and a spiritual awareness. We have taught you that the five pillars of Love are energetic states. Self-love is a by-product, a result of discovering that tuning yourself to these energy practices will naturally increase your Love for yourself. The tapping phrase from the emotional freedom technique that you use psychologically with self issues for healing the mind-body condition is, "Even though I fear [fill in the blank], I still Love and accept myself." This statement embodies both the self-love and the self-acceptance condition. Our focus now is on the Self-Love Stone to begin to create your foundation for daily living. We will explore self-love in a more concrete manner and also how it complements the energy practices.

> **Self-love is both a psychological condition and a spiritual awareness.**

The idea of Self-Love runs the spectrum from the negativity of destructive narcissism to the deep and positive power of self-worth. Self-love for your concerns addresses the feeling of shame, doubt, and self-judgment that you carry in your conscious and unconscious life. The first stone of Self-Love is the antidote for feeling that you are not enough, you are not capable, you are unworthy, or you are any other way that makes you feel in denial of who you are as a person.

When there is little Self-Love there is a condemnation and suppression of your fundamental nature as a human being. You shut off your feelings, your body sensations, and any avenue to nourish and care for yourself.

You substitute genuine Love for yourself with disguises of false humility on the one hand, to grandiose expressions of yourself on the other, to prove to others as well as yourself that you are okay to be alive. You develop reaction patterns that cover up your fear of being found out. You therefore project a mode of self-protection, self-control, dominance, reactions of anger, guilt, and/or self-rejection. You say to yourself, "I am no good. I am not enough. I will try harder. I didn't mean it. You don't understand; you are the one creating the problem, not me. I am in charge. Don't cross me." All these statements are strategies and emotional reactions to cover up self-hate and deep denial of your true essence as a human.

In your current culture, all psychological typing systems of personality and spiritual practices that try to work with behavioral issues and psycho-social therapies seek to address what we Three call the woven tapestry of your inner and outer projections; others call this the ego self. This tapestry you've woven together since birth is what you call your identity. As we described in the Five Pillars of Love your challenge and work is to release these woven, hard-wired patterns by using the projection of forgiveness and the other energy exercises that release the pattern of self-hate and rejection of your true self.

We continue to remind you to engage in the energetic practices, but also to recognize that self-love is a different embrace of one's identity while in a physical body. *To have genuine self-love is to discover within that you are the essence of light, and you are timeless and infinite space. In other words, there is no separation between your essence and the All of Existence.*

You truly will come to Love yourself by knowing and experiencing that this self you Love is actually Everything. Your identity is not confined to your separated body-mind. Rather, the self you Love is the eternal Self, not the ego identity you've constructed and projected into your three-dimensional world.

> **You truly will come to Love yourself by knowing and experiencing that this self you Love is actually Everything. Your identity is not confined to your separated body-mind. Rather, the self you Love is the eternal Self, not the ego identity you've constructed and projected into your three-dimensional world.**

Practice

There is a simple exercise for the Self-Love foundation stone that supports the energetic exercise of the Pillar of Forgiveness.

Each day take a concentrated, focused time of no more that 10 to 15 minutes and repeat to yourself "I Am That," to everything you see, feel, smell, taste, and touch. For several days do not name the thing you see, feel, smell, taste, or touch. Just say, "I Am That." Then, for a few days, name the thing. Notice the difference between naming and non-naming. The more you can non-name, the more your perception will expand to be that thing you are and experience that yourself is the Self of Everything.

Everything is you. Everything you experience in your life, both through your psychological perceptions and physical sensations, is this One Self. This Everything that you physically, emotionally, and mentally perceive is the essence of Love. This is the Love for yourself that you truly embrace. *Everything you experience in your life is the Self you Love. This Self is always mirroring back the Love of who you truly are.*

As you do the concentrated practice every day, you will find the awareness and projection of "I Am That" will naturally be present in all aspects of your life. You will naturally identify that the "other" is you. *A merging of your conscious awareness with the other will first happen. You will lose your "you" and then in time you will begin to experience just one awareness—just one consciousness—without separation or distinction between you and the other.* This is what many of your traditions call unity consciousness. In this unity consciousness, you Love the other as you Love yourself! No difference.

Remember, Self-Love is timeless, infinite in expression, and filled with the highest frequency of energy. This is the true identification with Self-Love. You Are That!

Humility

Foundation Stone Two

All the great beings of your planet learned the truth of humility. Many of these beings have been known through your histories. Most have simply lived private lives, learning and sharing with others within their natural circle of influence and caring. So what did these humble beings learn about humility?

These beings learned that humility is not a humbling of yourself. It is not something that you do or is done to you. Humbleness is not some demurring response to some action that is attributed to you. Humbleness does not come because you realized that what you may have achieved was fate or good fortune or dependent on many others who supported you and therefore you feel overwhelmed and humbled that somehow you received the grace of God.

You can often feel a range of feelings from unworthiness to deep appreciation in realizing that because of grace—because of some unmerited favor to you—you were able to do something you didn't think you were capable of doing, to be in the right place to solve a problem, to say the right thing to a person and thereby change their life, and so on. This we suggest is more a sense of gratitude than humility. When so-called *grace* happens, the sense of unworthiness can occur with the feeling, "I didn't deserve it, but somehow it happened to me." When grace isn't present for you, the attempts to help often can turn out badly and with it can come humiliation.

Humiliation is close to humility. To be humiliated is to be seen as one who was insufficient, the cause, the failure, or the unfortunate one. "I was humiliated by what I tried to do for that person that didn't work and then everyone turned on me for being so inappropriate." There is the positive so called humbleness coming from grace that happens and the negative humiliation from some poor attempt on your part. There is a fine line between the two circumstances, situations, or unforeseen events that often turn between the positive and the negative, between the pretense of humility and the humiliation of failure. You have experienced both of these and seen others who have experienced both.

What is true is that most people have not been in the presence of genuine humility. There is a phrase that runs through many of your spiritual traditions and religions: "Be like a hollow reed." This phrase embodies genuine humility. The essence of humility is that there is *nothing* in the person that is needed to be either humbled or humiliated when one is nothing. Life, both positive and negative, passes through the *hollow* nature of a person.

Being hollow means that there is no self to identify as being humble. Being hollow abides no resistance to what is occurring. Being hollow is being unattached to *any* outcome.

A *human reed* who is hollow still has a structure. Being hollow is a container for life. It has feelings, creativity, and energy that flows through its openness. In this sense, one as a hollow reed still has a personality, engages in work, activities, and relationships; but there is no forcing, no pushing against things, and no controlling of outcomes.

Besides the phrase of *hollow reed* there is another. The phrase is *hollow bones*. To have hollow bones is similar to being a hollow reed. It is to be open and fluid. A humble person's bones are hollow, open, receptive, and *dead to the flesh* of one's personality and ego.

A person of humility is hollow and there is a constant deep respect and gratitude that the Source of Existence constantly flows through them. When you meet a person of hollow-reed or hollow-bone humility, whether that person is a leader or a laborer, they are recognized by the sense of presence that reflects a different energy and responsiveness to life.

Here are the characteristics of hollow-reed humility:

1. You don't see an expressed defined personality. What is expressed is always fluid.
2. The person is not self-identified or separated from others.
3. They exhibit a joy, humor, and genuine interest in people, as well as a joy in the natural world and its beauty.
4. They can be exuberant as well as deeply quiet and contained.
5. They are respectful both of themselves and those around them.
6. They both listen and speak from a deep well of awareness about what is occurring in the moment.

These are the characteristics of true humility.

How do you practice humility? You don't. It is obvious from what we've described that humility is the result of something else. The key to understanding and experiencing humility is for you to become the hollow reed—to become the hollow bone. Becoming the hollow reed is a life-long process. If you are on this journey of awakening to your essential nature, much of the process is simply cleaning out the hollow part of the reed of one's life. The more clearing of the inner reed then the hollower you become, so that the Energy of Life passes through you without resistance.

First Practice

This hollowing out of you is a natural process. Everyone who is choosing to awaken perceives what is blocking, resisting, or holding them back from this great energetic flow that they sense and also experience from time to time.

The questions for you are these:

1. What choice will you make today to clear yourself?
2. How much pain and resistance will you endure to keep doing what blocks you?
3. Of what must you let go to have more space in your life?
4. And, what is it that you must now embrace that you fear to accept into your life?

These and many more questions are your daily investigation to clean and clear and become a hollow being. Here are two more.

1. Write out one question at the beginning of the day and write an answer at the end of the day.
2. Some days just sit and contemplate, chew on the questions and ASK a Source greater than yourself for insight.

Since becoming a hollow reed is a continual process, there is no end result that you are seeking. It is not that the reed becomes clean and hollow once and for all and now you've arrived. The focus is not simply to clean and clear out and simply be hollow. Rather, the magic of the hollow reed is that it becomes bigger and bigger and expands in size and shape so that there is a larger tube for more flow to move through it. As you become more expanded and hollow you will experience more grace. Grace is this natural flood of energy from the Source of Existence that brings through your forgiveness, compassion, kindness, appreciation, and gratitude, which are the essential characteristics of the heart of Love.

Second Practice

Let us give you now a two-part practice that can be used throughout your lifetime to become a hollow reed.

At some time every day, ask yourself the following questions:

1. What am I *resisting* right now?
2. About what am I *unwilling* to make a choice?
3. What am I *frightened* to let go of?
4. What do I want to take action on, but feel *stuck*?

As a way to remember these questions use the four letters RUFS (for *Resisting, Unwilling, Frightened, Stuck*) to keep them daily in your awareness.

There are other similar questions you can ask, but what you want to observe in yourself and ask yourself is this: *what today is blocking my becoming a hollow reed?*

1. **The first step** then is to observe and question what is blocking the flow of your life right now. This is awareness without judging yourself.

    Don't treat any blocks you observe psychologically.

    Simply observe them with awareness. Don't try to figure out why it's a block or what you should do about clearing it. You may observe several blocks, but just note them.

2. **The second step** is to mentally bring the block(s) to your heart and breathe into the block(s).

    Let yourself relax into the resisting blocks by just noticing them.

What you will find is that some blocks will naturally appear to dissolve on their own as you breathe. You will know they are dissolving because there is a feeling of space and peace in you after they disappear. Other blocks will remain as you continue to breathe at the heart.

After breathing into the blocks continue to keep them at your heart and then focus on visualizing or sensing warm energy coming up from the earth to the base of your spine and then up the spine to your heart with the flow of the energy moving the resisting block(s) up through the remainder of your spine, out the top of your head into the eighth chakra, a foot or so above your head. Just feel, see, sense, and know that these block(s) have disappeared into this vast field of energy.

Continue feeling this flow of earth energy moving through you up and out the top of your head. This is the feeling of you becoming the hollow reed.

Once again, the process of becoming a hollow reed begins with your awareness of the resisting block(s) and releasing them by

1. putting your attention on your breath at the heart with pulsating energy,
2. creating a flow of energy from the earth up the spine as you move the blocks out the top of the head, and
3. experiencing the blocks being naturally dissolved and resolved in the vastness of the energy as it flows up through you from the earth.

Depending on the nature of your blocks, repeat the process as many times as you need. There will come a point where you know the block(s) are gone. If there is a choice, or action, or a movement to let go, as an outward manifestation in your life, it will happen quite naturally and easily. *Please remember, don't force yourself to become hollow.*

What is blocking my becoming a hollow reed today?

Self-Acceptance

Foundation Stone Three

Self-acceptance is clearly connected to self-love. Self-love, as we indicated, is the releasing of the psycho-spiritual identity structure that you developed and created as compensation for the environmental conditions of your life pattern circumstances. These are the energy patterns that you brought into this life from other existences. The work of self-love is to expand yourself beyond this woven tapestry of self-protective identity. The Foundation Stone of Self-Love is expansion beyond what you psychologically call your ego structure. Thus, we gave you the foundation practice of *I Am That*. This practice opens and expands the dimensions of your awareness to directly experience the vastness of the Love that is your core essence. The you that *You* really are is not the self-protective shield you've created; rather, it is the essence of Everything!

Whereas self-love is expansion, self-acceptance is limitation. This is a startling view of strange opposites. The statement you often combine together is "I Love and accept myself"; this mirrors these opposites. These opposites are like the breath function of expanding and contracting, of inhalation and exhalation. What we would emphasize in this comparison is that self-love is the inhalation of filling, expanding, and opening to Love within you.

Self-acceptance as exhalation is the release, the coming back, the relaxation, the softening, the pulling within, the setting of boundaries, and the awareness of natural limitations that bring you to rest and finally to peace.

> **Whereas in self-love you expand into space, in self-acceptance you release yourself from the pressure of time.**

Self-acceptance is discovering your own rhythm living in this three-dimensional world. Whereas in self-love you expand into space, in self-acceptance you release yourself from the pressure of time. Time and space are complementary opposites. In the five pillars of Love, we discussed learning to move into higher frequencies of energy in order to go beyond time into the vastness of space. For your daily psycho-spiritual life, we are giving you foundation stones that complement the energy work in more practical and grounded ways.

This Foundation Stone of Self-Acceptance alters time for you. To not accept who you are is to be caught in the time of continual tension, high stress, unresolved anxiety, a lack of confidence, deep self-judgment, perfectionism, a negative image of yourself, and so on. All you have to do is stop for a moment and notice the negative self-talk you have for yourself. *The negative self-talk characteristics are the false limitations that keep the mind, heart, and body constricted and unable to discover the natural movement, flow, and expression of your life.* Because of false identity and constricted behavioral and emotional pain, you fundamentally do not accept the enormous potential, creativity, joy and, most of all, the peace of simply being what you were created to be.

To exhale your breath is to release whatever constricts you. The exhale lets you come to rest, settles you into a different configuration of energy in your body. This is perceived as the relaxation of your emotions, a settling and quieting of your feelings, and a naturally slowing of your inner mind chatter. Letting the air out of your body, emotions, and mind is what brings you to a potential place of peacefulness, deep relaxation, and rest.

It is in this peaceful resting place of body, heart, and mind where you will experience true self-acceptance. Self-acceptance is being at rest and at peace with whatever is occurring in your body, mind, and heart. In *contracting* into inner peace, you break up the power of time over your life with all its demands, pressures, fears, anxieties, and stresses.

Utilizing self-love and self-acceptance as complementary opposites will break you out of the constraints of your false identity to experience the increasing expansion within you of both space and timelessness. *Self-love moves you into the expansion of the Everything of "I Am That." With self-acceptance you are going in the opposite direction to experience the release of anything you give to the condition of time.* You break through the knothole of time to discover the eternal still point of peace. This is the peace that is described in your Bible as *The peace that passes all understanding.*

So, again, self-love breaks through the identity into the space of absolute Love that you are. Self-acceptance breaks through the false self's control of time to move down, back, and into that still point of absolute peace. *Love and Peace are the outcome of these complementary opposites.*

From this place of stillness and peace you have clarity, insight, direct knowledge, and the continual awareness of life being lived by its own natural rhythm, pace, flow, and expression. Behavioral patterns, action intentions, emotional expression, and mental acuity naturally expand and contract four characteristics: rhythm, pace, flow, and expression. *To live in this awareness of life, breathe in and out thoughts and feelings of harmony, balance, and sensitivity for yourself and everyone and everything around you.*

Many people like you have practiced meditation of some form. You can recognize the state condition and experience of living daily from this still point of peace within you. The happy discovery for most of you is that living from this still point of peace, the Life Force within you moves you, rather than you self-directing, forcing, or generating an action that is not natural to the movement of your own rhythm.

> So, again, self-love breaks through the identity into the space of absolute Love that you are. Self-acceptance breaks through the false self's control of time to move down, back, and into that still point of absolute peace.

First Practice

The practice stone of self-acceptance is both simple and challenging. It is in two parts.

The First Practice is almost mandatory for everyone in order to come to the still point of inner peace. To learn and experience this inner peace and outer rhythm, you must practice some form of meditation. The practice is every day. You cannot break the hold of time and its accompanying pressures and constraints if you don't learn to daily quiet your body, heart, and mind.

All your traditional spiritual paths point to meditation as the doorway to discovering the natural expression of your life here in this world at this chaotic moment in your history. Meditation is the breaking down of the construction of your false identity. It is this identity that keeps you from living from the still point of peace.

1. The most basic meditation practice is to follow the inhale and exhale of your breathing. Whenever your mind drifts, don't judge yourself; simply bring your attention back to the breath. Over time, the mind settles like the calming of the waves on a lake into a smooth reflecting mirror.
2. If you already have a meditation practice, get serious about consistently doing it for twenty minutes to an hour each day.

Second Practice

Beyond the practice of daily meditation is to connect to the rhythms of the natural world. This is an observing practice.

1. Sit or walk in the woods or a park, or in your backyard, or look through your window at the trees, birds, clouds, sun, or whatever you see, smell, hear, and feel.
2. Let your breath begin to slow with the sense of what you are seeing, hearing, and feeling. Most of all, let your awareness rest in this opening of your senses to this experience of life around you. This is an experience of life not being lived according to your sense of time, but rather being lived in harmony with what is actually occurring.
3. The challenge of this practice is to make time in your life to do this observing, breathing, and resting in the natural world of slower rhythms. *Just as meditation will give you a deepening and clearer awareness, this practice will do the same to bring you to the still point of inner peace as you engage in the world.*

Both practices complement each other. The meditation practice is shutting out the world around you to go within. The observing practice is to open up a different rhythm in you by moving out of yourself into a rhythm with the natural world.

Third Practice

This is about how you tend to rush and push your life. This is an important practice for the time in which you live. Too often your rhythm is to force time, to rush to do things quickly, to try to discover ways to have more time, and to try to get more done in less time. This pressure of putting more energy into a limited amount of time generates pressure and tension in your body, in emotions such as fear and anxiety. As well you become future focused mentally so you are not feeling, experiencing, and knowing the rhythm of each of your actions. You escape in this way so as to not be present and aware of yourself and how your body, mind, and heart complement each other. All three parts of your being must be united to slip past the control and prison of time. The deep unconscious pattern for you and almost everyone in your society is fearing you will run out of time. This means you fear your ending, your death. When your reality is stuck in the perception that there is only birth and death, time dominates. When time is compressed into the moment, you discover eternity and the endless place of beauty, awareness, and where everything is possible.

Discovering the present moment is to discover freedom within you. Loving self-acceptance is simply being in this moment that has no time. You can only accept what you are—eternal in this moment and then the next moment and the next.

Here is the third practice, which helps you know there is simplicity in observing one thing at a time. This is how to experience the moment.

1. Observe something: a leaf on a tree, a lizard on a rock, a bird at a feeder, a cloud in the sky, a baby sleeping, a dog eating food, the sunlight through a window, or anything else that attracts your attention. Just narrow your attention down to one thing.
2. Focus all your senses on this thing. Obviously, observe with your eyes, but also listen, smell, and where appropriate touch and feel, for example, the fur of a cat or dog. Lightly touch the skin on your hand or other parts of your body. Focus on each sensation in turn.
3. While observing with each of your sensors, become aware of your heart. Bring each sensation to your heart and feel appreciation for what you are experiencing.
4. Each focus on sensation will lead you moment-by-moment into peace and serenity. Each moment, let your being rest in your heart, following its gentle rhythm.

Each of these practices opens a deep doorway of self-acceptance.

Reflection

Foundation Stone Four

Reflection is a psychological, metaphorical, and practical way in which you lead your life. Reflection is looking into a mirror and contemplating what you see there. Reflection mirrors back your projections about yourself and the creation of your world. *But for our purposes, reflection is a remembering that acts to release the patterns and mirrors of your life.*

The word *reflection* means that someone or a situation or some external or internal awareness is mirroring back to you the experiences and patterns of your life, as well as your thoughts, behaviors, and actions. What you think, feel, emote, verbally express, act on, and intuit is reflecting your state of being at any moment. It mirrors what is reality for you.

A positive notion of reflection as an act of contemplation is a way of considering and exploring your experience, action, behavior, and thought. To reflect and contemplate some thing is to pause and look into its nature, effect, process, and movement in your life. Further, contemplation is to consider and look from different angles, vantage points, and ways of understanding what you are examining.

> **What you think, feel, emote, verbally express, act on, and intuit is reflecting your state of being at any moment. It mirrors what is reality for you.**

Pause in your reading and consider the following questions as a means to contemplate issues in your life.

1. In your life at this moment, what issue, concern, person, action, or situation is *dominating* your thoughts, feelings, and experience?
2. What *impact* does this situation or circumstance have on you, others, and your inner and outer life?
3. In what way do you feel most *vulnerable* in this situation or experience?
4. How does the *process* of what is occurring in you, by being vulnerable, drive your thoughts, feeling, and actions?
5. How does the *interaction* of your thoughts, feelings, actions, and/or behaviors with this issue impact your life in positive or negative ways?
6. Is there anything you can do in this moment to *alter* the situation you are contemplating?

It is useful to write out your responses to these questions as you reflect and contemplate them. The more you write, the more insights and understanding begin to emerge for you. Use these questions as jumping off points for reflecting and contemplating on what is occurring in your life, particularly what is troubling you about yourself or others.

The nature and means of how you reflect on your life leads also to how your projection and/or reflection cast their images out onto the world and how you will perceive the image of yourself and others. In your development, growth, and deepening as a human identity, you need reflection and contemplation in order to observe the projections and effects of your life on others and the world. You then need to determine how you turn these projections inward to create your identity as a self. *Reflecting on this outward and inward projection process provides the nexus point of transformation.*

You have heard it said that everything is a mirror reflecting back to you the nature of your reality. This is true. These dimensions of reflecting we've described are what operate in every human. However, in most people this reflecting on oneself and the world is mostly unconscious. Those who contemplate deeply and concentratedly and those who are skillful at meditation can break through the mirrors to experience reality directly.

We have described in the Five Pillars of Love that your identity is a woven tapestry of projections. For most of you, reflecting is observing your projections and what they reflect back to you and, therefore, how they reinforce your woven identity. At some point you may begin to work at the energetic level to try to break up these projections and unravel your identity tapestry by seeing through the mirrors you've created. Meditation comes the closest to doing this, along with specific energy exercises to change the dynamics of the reinforcing of the mirrors that your projections set up and reflect back to you, as we have indicated before.

However, with this explanation we want to give you a means to crack open these reflecting mirrors in another way. Unless you can break through your house of mirrors, all your projections reflecting back to you the illusory construct of your reality will continue. Without cracking your mirrors, you will never experience true freedom in this life. *Breaking through the self-reinforcing reflections that make up who and what you think you are, is the central purpose of liberation in this lifetime.* And, yes, we know what you are thinking. Your question is, "How do I break through the reflecting and reinforcing mirrors of my identity? And, how do I break through the personal and general consensus reality I live within? And finally, how do I create this breakthrough to experience liberation and freedom?"

As a foundation stone for daily living, cracking the reflection of yourself is achieved by a particular daily practice. From the moment of your birth you've been constructing your identity and the world you live in. Both your identity and your world is different from everyone else's, even though you with others conspire to create a consensus reality that is constantly changing. *Other than a core breakdown mentally and emotionally, the only way to deconstruct a life of projections and reinforcing reflections from the world around you is to apply energetic processes to your being on a daily basis.* The energy exercises in the Five Pillars of Love are indeed part of this daily practice along with some of the other energy exercises we've given to you. However, there is a core exercise that acts as a key lever to produce the needed crack in the mirrors of your life. This exercise is deceptively simple. Here is the context for it.

The projections that make up your identity and experience of your world come from your thoughts and the patterning of those thoughts. Thoughts overlap and weave together the patterns of your experience as being real to you. *The purpose of this exercise we are giving you is to pull out the threads of these woven patterns and produce an unraveling of your perceptions of yourself and your reality system. When this unraveling happens the reinforcing and reflecting mirrors break apart and you experience reality as it actually is.* This practice helps pull apart the false self you've created.

Practice

Every morning in your meditation time and then separately as many times as you remember throughout the day, do the following:

1. Focus your attention at your forehead region. Feel the forehead energy getting warm and pulsating as you concentrate on it.

2. As the focus of energy builds at your forehead center, say to yourself the following: *"I release all thoughts, memories, and emotions that created my life and my world."*
3. Repeat this phrase several times as you keep the energy focus on your forehead.
4. At a comfortable point, bring this energy down to your heart area and repeat the following: *"Love is my essence. All that I am is Love."* Feel the warm pulsating energy at the heart as you say this phrase. Repeat this phrase a number of times.
5. Do this practice many times throughout the day. The more you do the practice the more you unravel and break through the mirrors that keep you from the Truth of reality and the nature of your True Self.

Don't hurry as you repeat these two phrases at the forehead and the heart. *Feel the energy strongly at the forehead and caressingly at the heart.* The more you slowly practice, the more you experience yourself as the source of your essential and true nature. This practice takes just a few minutes, but through continued application, observe how you become more aware, open, spacious, and less controlled by your old patterns and perceptions. *Reflection is about releasing the image of your identity and the image of the world you created to protect yourself.* The intention in the exercise is to continually release the threads of thought, memory, and emotion that created your false self and your world, and then to affirm your true essence that is the energy of Love. Remember to recite many times throughout the day, "Love is my essence. All that I am is Love."

Let this be so in you.

Release of Old Patterns

Foundation Stone Five

*I*n the foundation stone of Reflection you were given the practice to break through the illusion of the mirrors that reflected back your false identity and that of the world you created to protect yourself. This new foundation stone of Release of Old Patterns is not only to release the thoughts, memories, and emotions that created your identity and world that you practice in Reflection but is also to take another step. *This step is to release the fundamental patterns from your ancestral past and the probable future that make up your attachment to your civilization patterns.*

Releasing old patterns from the past or creating negative patterns for the future is not just about you personally. The energetic forces that hold together the continuity of your personal ancestral line and your current cultural line bakes into your experience a perceived reality that is false and constraining as to how you are to really live in three-dimensional time-space. Your false self creates constant resistance and false mirrors of self-protection that keep you in isolation and fear. Your society and your world civilization as a whole are constantly resisting the flow of the energy of Love through all beings. Your civilization has been weaving the threads of deep delusion, fear, pain, and destruction of the natural world. We will explain that these destructive patterns not only come from choices from the past but also from the future. As you learn to release these patterns of past and future you are part of transforming the structural reality of the current space-time experience you are living within.

We said in the introduction to the Five Foundation Stones for Daily Living that it is important to follow and practice the sequence in which we give you these five foundation stones. The Reflection stone is based on personal transformation of cracking the mirrors of your self-made identity and the structure of how you perceive your life and world. Reflection is a necessary step of release at the personal level. Whenever your practice begins to transform your experience of reality and as realization occurs in you, the natural process is to begin to transform the reality of everything around you in your present world.

> **So-called primitive cultures knew that everything is happening simultaneously and *bleeding* back and forth through all the past and future realities.**

Let us examine how you begin to function and release old negative patterns that extend back in time. We begin with your ancestors. In many spiritual traditions, particularly in Indigenous peoples, rituals and ceremonies are carried out by individuals as well as groups who seek to heal and restore the balance and harmony in the generational relationships. These peoples knew that the choices and decisions of peoples seven generations back from them would have either positive or negative impact on their current lives and society. If a generation is approximately twenty-five years long, then the impact from the past and on future generations needed to be considered in terms of 175 years. In making decisions, their shamans and healers would go outside time and look back and then forward to observe what impact their current decisions had on the future as well as the past. They would also look to see what decisions future generations would be making that would impact them in their present time. In your world of linear thought you only perceive in one direction. In these so-called primitive cultures they knew that everything is happening simultaneously and *bleeding* back and forth through all the past and future realities.

Both your individual and societal impact on the future conditions of people needs to be considered over this 175-year pattern. Considering the patterns you see at play today and the choices or non-choices people around you and in leadership and power are making, the question becomes, "What do you think your world will be like in 175 years, or even twenty-five or fifty years?" When you stand at this fulcrum point as an individual or as a group of people or as the civilization itself, every choice and decision you and others make will have a huge ripple effect going forward. You know this intellectually, but you have not taken the implications into your heart and deeper feelings. By your thoughts, behaviors, and actions, you constantly change today and, by your choices, you change the future for millions if not billions of people.

In the Five Pillars of Love, we emphasized compassion and kindness as the basis for thought, behavior, and action. With this foundation stone of releasing old patterns, we are encouraging you to take these qualities of compassion and kindness into the chaos of your current world and release the engrained patterns that hold back the evolutionary growth of humanity to awaken to a higher energetic vibration level of existence.

Many previous civilizations on your planet have come to a similar point of transformation and died in the chrysalis, never emerging, as the butterfly does, to a higher plane of experience. *The question before your civilization is whether you go the same way, always trying to change but never taking the next step of evolutionary transformation.* We are confident that within the growing chaos, individuals and groups can be forces that release the blocked energy of previous generations of their negative choices, decisions, and actions. The last pivot point of the previous seventh generation that has influence on your current situation began around 1840 to 1850. This was the beginning era of your industrial revolution and the beginning of the machine age as you know it today. From steam engine to gold rush, from massacring native people to clearing virgin forests, and from expansion through war and the attempt to stop slavery, the underlying energy of this period was greed without regard for humanity or nature. We need not recite a litany of many other poor-to-bad decisions, choices, and actions from this period of time that bring us to the chaos of your world today with its greed, corruption, destruction of nature, and control over people's lives. You see the results of this past time period all around you.

If you work on the foundation stone of your own release, it naturally begins to move you to want to help release what is destroying so many people, communities, and ultimately your natural world. This is the intent of this foundation stone. Outwardly what you see with your mirrored eyes seems hopeless to stop or change. You believe there is so little of what you really know or understand in this complex, chaotic world. This is true, but just as you wove a tapestry of a false self and found that you could pull the threads of this tapestry apart to be able to perceive life as it actually is, so too can you pull apart the woven, false civilization culture that is destroying your world. By explaining this foundation stone, we want to help you change your belief and your perception by going back seven generations to heal a false view of life. And, we want to teach you to go forward seven generations into the future to heal what your civilization today is bringing into existence for that time. In healing the past and the future, you heal the present. You pull apart the woven tapestry of a false and destructive civilization that keeps repeating itself. *Today you can help lay the groundwork for a truly evolutionary and transformational leap into an entirely different dimension of reality.*

We give you this framework in order to know that the practices we are giving you in this foundation stone are the basis of all your true spiritual traditions. Many traditions have practices to bring healing, salvation, and transformation to all humanity and all beings: the notion of prophets, saviors, and saints to help you gain salvation in the monotheistic traditions; the bodhisattva tradition in Buddhism to bring all beings to enlightenment; the energy traditions of the Taoists to use the body to transform one's life; the Hindu gods that help all beings flourish through many incarnations; and the vast age of shamanism that sought to balance and harmonize all beings, human and non-human. This foundation stone of Release of Old Patterns is another in this line of traditions.

Two Practices

We are giving you two practices that are strong energetic forces capable of effecting both time and space. That is, these two practices can transform the time and space of the past and the time and space of the future.

First Practice

The first practice is freeing the pattern of your past through the lineage of your family ancestors and your general understanding of the previous seven generations from around the 1840s time period.

1. The first step is to make a list of your lineage via both parents, going back to grandparents, great grandparents and if needed

to great, great grandparents. If you don't know your actual lineage, read something about the 1840 to 1850 time period in the United States as well as in other places in the world at that time. Those of you in the United States could imagine emigrants coming from other places in the world to your country. There was an influx of emigrants from Europe, Asia, Africa, and Latin America. As industrialization began, there were the beginning of factories and the building of cities in Europe and North America. Huge changes began that affect your world today. This first step gives you a personal context to the choices and decisions that affect you and everyone else in the world today.

2. The second step is to create a table, shelf, or floor corner in your home that has pictures of your lineage and/or pictures of this 1840-to-1850 period. Also, place a favorite stone, a bird feather, a small bowl of water, and a candle around the pictures. These are the four elements—earth, air, water, and fire. This is an ancestral altar. It is a traditional and concrete reminder of both the humans and the natural world ancestors that you care about.

3. The third step is to sit once a day before the altar at least for fifteen minutes doing a specific releasing process.

4. The fourth step as you sit in front of your altar is to bring energy from the earth up your spine to your heart, and then draw down energy from the cosmos through the crown of your head to your heart. At the heart, breathe rapidly, pulsing the energy to grow in your heart. This pulsing of energy should be familiar from other energy practices within the Five Pillars of Love.

5. The fifth step is concentrating on and strengthening the energy at your heart. Then put your attention on your ancestors and the pictures of the middle 1800s. Now direct your heart energy like a beam of light into that period of time filling your ancestors and all human choices, decisions, and activities with this

energy of Love. Hold the intention that all the negative energy and poor choices are released from that time period. Hold the intention of this energy until you feel a release into a sense of inner peace. In your heart, hold no judgment, only caring, kindness, compassion, and Love. Do this practice for one month every day and you will begin to perceive some amazing transformations in your lineage that bring you and them healing. It will also bring healing to the world around you now.

Second Practice

The second practice is to work with releasing the future just as the first practice was working to release the past. In this practice, you will step outside of time and look into the future that is being determined by the events and choices of today. This movement into the future is not pretending or creating a make-believe experience. We will help you to open yourself to a superordinate dimension of reality that is available to you if you are willing to work with energy and consistently do the practices that take you outside time and space. All it takes is a willingness to let go and release your old patterns.

1. The first step is to set your awareness for 175 years into future time. This would be approximately 2190 to 2200.

2. The second step is to once again bring the energy of the earth and the cosmos into your heart. Breathe deeply, pulsate, and feel the buildup of energy in your heart. When the energy is very strong in your heart, move the energy up the spine and out the crown of your head. Feel your awareness move freely from your body and set your intention to move forward to 2200.

3. The third step is to keep focused on a timeline moving forward into the future. One way to do this is by counting the years

in increments of twenty-five years. At each twenty-five-year point, note the feeling and even the visual changes of that period as you go through the segments of approximately 2050, 2075, 2100, and so on. When you get to 2200, let yourself rest and be open to whatever you perceive through your senses. You may have images, sensations in your body, emotions, and more. Simply note them.

4. The fourth step is to do something very important. ASK a Source greater than yourself to bring energy, light, peace, harmony, balance, and whatever else is needed for healing and change to this time through your heart. It is your heart energy that you are sending forward from your time into this future time to release whatever needs to be let go so that there is a different future than what is being created today. If you do this daily for a month you will learn an enormous amount and experience the power of timeless transformation.

It is your willingness to practice this exercise that will deepen your experience of being part of healing the past and future by releasing negative and destructive patterns from your civilization.

May you be faithful to this practice on behalf of all beings on your planet in your past, present, and future.

Working with Your Practice

First Comment

One morning when I was reading the introduction to the "Stones" and the various sections, I noted that the Three had indicated in the introduction that they would present how to combine the practices of the "Pillars" with the "Stones" after presenting all five foundation stone practices. I asked if they were still going to give me that material. Their response was both personal to me but also general for anyone beginning to work with both sets of practices. After receiving the answer to my question, I asked if I could put this material in the manuscript as I felt it would be useful to others beside myself. They said yes. I give you below the transcription as I received it.

> David, we are glad that you are being more consistent in working with the practices of both the Pillars and the Stones. At this moment in time, we suggest that you intuitively work with one or the other of the practices in each section. What is important for you is how you need to work different issues and dimensions of your life at different times. So, today, work with the *I Am That* practice in the Self-Love Stone.
>
> Do not underestimate how these practices work on your mind, body, and heart. A practice is a practice. Trust your practice.

A practice shapes a container for you to pull apart the threads of your woven tapestry. A practice also recreates and moves you into your essence at the same time. This is both the mystery of practice and the means of transformation and transcendence of your existence here in this dimension. The practices are teaching you to be at inner peace by energizing your capacity to be in the fifth dimension. Yes, both the Pillars and the Stones are to bring you into the fifth-dimensional experience. The fifth dimension is on the other side of what you will experience as physical death. When you begin to experience the fifth dimension while you are in physical form, the passage through the doorway of death will hold little fear or concern for you.

Just as you've asked us earlier, your practice today is *I Am That*. It teaches that there is no *you* that can be identified as a *you*. The true reality is that *Everything Is You*. This practice will teach you this and help shape your container to know this truth. But to experience being Everything is both a release and an embrace of your essence, which is Love and, therefore, what Everything is. So also include the Reflection practice as it works with you letting go of your thoughts, memories, and emotions so as to experience your true essence of Love. These words in the practices hold little meaning until you fully experience what we've been teaching you and providing for you to experience in the practices.

Second Comment

After the Three gave me this material, I asked them to summarize the use of practices for others who read these comments. This is what follows.

So, for all who may read this, know that you must trust your intuition and ask within yourself what practices and combination of practices between the Five Pillars and the Five Foundation Stones you should be working with at any given time in order to take your natural next step of inner and outer development. First, we remind you that you should work individually with all the practices first and then begin to combine them together. For example, there are natural combinations such as Compassion from the Five Pillars and Release of Old Patterns from the Five Foundation Stones. You will discover these combinations for yourself as you work with the material we've given.

As you continue the practices, there will be incremental shifts of awareness, understanding, and direct knowing. And then, there will be leaps. You, David, haven't made a leap yet, but the continuing practices will build the energetic platform from where the only alternative and the natural next step is to leap. That leap can help all of you who read this to learn to change dimensions, which is beyond anything you currently know.

Enough for now. Know you are *That*.

> **As you continue the practices, there will be incremental shifts of awareness, understanding, and direct knowing. And then, there will be leaps. You, David, haven't made a leap yet, but the continuing practices will build the energetic platform from where the only alternative and the natural next step is to leap. That leap can help all of you who read this to learn to change dimensions, which is beyond anything you currently know.**

The Challenges of the End Times

Now, in regard to this last part of our *Energy Teachings*, this part we entitle the Challenges of the End Times, let us first provide a short introduction. We present here four sections along with exercises to awaken a deeper, larger understanding and experience of the transition and transformation of your planet and civilization and what you are experiencing at this time in your history.

We say to all who read this last part of the book that we are presenting this material not to frighten you. We do it rather to both inspire and encourage your inner soul awareness to come to a greater understanding of yourself as an individual, as well as a greater understanding of the collective role in this time of change, the disintegration of old patterns of thinking, and new ways of being in your daily life.

For any individual or group of individuals to survive and thrive during this unraveling of your individual and societal life patterns, you must confront the deepest part of your soul awareness and release the woven tapestry of your ego structure. The first two parts of the book address these concerns. Let us now provide an overview, which many of you already perceive.

What you experience all around and in the world at large is the destructive technologies, the authoritarian social systems, and the lack of humane values to guide the direction of a society. There is also the lack of guidance to cultivate an inner life that connects you and fellow humans to realms and dimensions of experience that ultimately are the reality of your natural inheritance. These conditions are some of the reasons that are causing your civilization to break apart at this time. However, the breaking apart is not just attributable to these current conditions. The patterns of this breakdown have been developing intensely for the past five hundred years throughout the world. It is your industrial revolution of a hundred and fifty years ago that intensely accelerated the condition of your civilization to the point it is in at this time.

Everything that humans have developed over the past ten thousand years leads to the extreme imbalance that is destroying the natural world, especially through the overpopulation by humans. The devising of extreme instruments of war and authoritarian control may in fact reduce the planet to a level of destruction where humans and most animal life will be gone. Whether this happens in total or part will be the result of the collective insanity dominating your lives in the next several years. Many clear thinking and feeling individuals see what is coming. In fact, many are shouting the warning, but few will listen, and fewer still know what to do or how to personally or collectively respond.

Throughout your world there are pockets of individuals and groups that are beginning to prepare for this devastation. Our message to you who read this is that we want you to come into an inner knowing and inner listening, and be assisted by the understanding and practices that we will provide to help you become part of the transformation and evolution of your species. We seek to help you come into harmony, balance, and deep connection with all beings who inhabit this realm called earth.

The greatest challenge for each of you will be to learn how to transcend the fear, turmoil, chaos, and destruction that is the harbinger of what has evolved many times on your planet. In the far distant past, humanity came to this crisis point and failed many times. It takes hundreds of thousands of years to evolve a civilization that permits a species to transcend its physical form and step into a reality system that is expansive and interconnected to all beings and energy forms. Within the evolution of your world civilization, your mystics and advanced teachers have evolved to this point of transformation, but the step beyond them has not permeated into the larger population. When this penetration of teaching and experience does not occur in a civilization, the individual isolation creates ego structural dominance and usually ends as it is ending in this period of time you now live in. As you have experienced, the ego essentially separates and covers itself with a tapestry of self-protection. Individuals and cultures weave around themselves their technology and social buffers of separation and dominance. This separation promotes the dominance of males over females and of humans over the environment, and the destruction of one another in war for economic gain and power.

The greatest challenge for each of you will be to learn how to transcend the fear, turmoil, chaos, and destruction that is the harbinger of what has evolved many times on your planet.

The opportunity and challenge for you is to let go of your isolating life. Renounce your seeming abandonment and isolation, not just at a physical level, but at a metaphysical level. Let go in order to discover within you a release of your ego tapestry and experience an expansion of awareness. This release guides you, keeps you from anxiety and fear, and opens the channels of Love, kindness, gratitude, and compassion for yourself and others. In doing this work, you will be guided to affirming groups that will provide a circle of energy, and a place to develop your spiritual gifts and safety in the turmoil. The practices we have given in the first two parts of the book will assist you to be able to survive and thrive through the increasing storm.

> **The opportunity and challenge for you is to let go of your isolating life. Renounce your seeming abandonment and isolation, not just at a physical level, but at a metaphysical level. Let go in order to discover within you a release of your ego tapestry and experience an expansion of awareness.**

In the following four sections, we will outline the nature of the times you are now facing and what will lie ahead for you and your world.

We will provide the meaning for why there will be such significant changes environmentally on the planet.

Ultimately, we want you to understand the spiritual meaning of endings and beginnings and how these two happen simultaneously.

Finally, the last section will focus on the promise or possibility of a new world, and a new pattern of living together on the planet. We will speak of the emergence of the awakening of a truly human entity who embodies a new awareness and perception of reality.

In each of these sections we will provide practices appropriate to your development and the conditions and circumstances you may individually experience.

Let us begin with the Nature of Times Ahead.

The Nature of Times Ahead

Understanding the First Challenge

It is very easy for anyone who has some degree of awareness that the conditions in the world are extremely challenging and disconcerting. People all over the world are being driven into two separate frames of existence. There are those privileged enough to live in economic societies that function reasonably well and those who live in poverty, war, famine, weather and earth devastation, and/or are under severe political and social dominance. Both the privileged and the underprivileged will increasingly face the breakdown and collapse of a functioning society that will lead to a life that could not be considered normal in any sense of that word.

What is increasingly difficult and producing great harm and suffering is the growing weather and environmental destruction. The destructive climate conditions will be a growing phenomenon of the world. Terrible conditions of extraordinary environmental catastrophe will increase. In many countries, the rise of authoritarianism and the beginning of civil internal warfare will escalate as people divide up around ideological belief systems to seek safety and security from their leaders.

For many people, these times appear to dramatize the end days as described in your Bible and in many other prophetic documents in different religions and societies around your world. But these end days are also being described by scientists as unprecedented temperatures from global warming will increase worldwide, with massive hurricanes, earthquakes, rapidly melting ice in the Arctic and Antarctica, rising ocean-water levels flooding coastal cities, creating fire and droughts and destruction in cities, as well as limited food supplies throughout the world.

Knowing that societies and earth conditions are breaking down and wreaking havoc on people around the world, what does all this mean for you now and in the near future?

Let it be understood that these conditions—particularly those linked to climate change that produce suffering from fire, floods, hurricanes, drought, and famine—are the result of a lack of positive and humane choices and the lack of genuine caring for others and the environment. All this suffering has not just come in the last 150 years of industrialization; it has been developing for centuries.

Most of you reading this book know these things we've described because you are experiencing them. What is needed from you now is how you personally and in the particular society that you live in have contributed to this growing destruction and political and social upheaval that is creating massive fear and reactive actions.

> **Knowing that societies and earth conditions are breaking down and wreaking havoc on people around the world, what does all this mean for you now and in the near future?**

Preparing to Practice

Our first practice before we continue this discussion is to have you stop reading and explore the following questions and self-reflections. You may not have full answers or considerations for these questions and reflections, but we will prompt you in the days ahead to muse on them and explore your part in order to release the unconscious patterns that connect you to the larger pattern creating the current conditions of collapse and destruction. As you consider these questions, know that we are present with you. Your response to these questions is not a judgement upon you; rather it is a means to release the unconscious threads in your ego tapestry.

1. *What beliefs and judgements have you made about yourself and others as you've perceived and absorbed* the decaying situation in the world? What is your *response and reaction* toward the people who surround your life and the way they respond to what is occurring?
2. *Do you feel yourself as tight and frozen,* looking at "things" so that everything—people, animals, trees, lakes, countries, and more—have little to no impact on you because they too are just "things" to interact with or avoid?
3. *Do you have a floating anxiety* that you may get caught, for example, in a fire or hurricane? Or that someone could suddenly shoot you in a store or school for no reason? *Do you live with growing fear* that you are never safe?
4. *Do you blot out* the news and events around you? Or *are you consumed* by the media? Or *do you pretend* that nothing will happen to you?

This first series of question lets you consider how much you are really in fear, denial, and/or cutting yourself off from the world around you by absorbing yourself in sublimating experiences such as TV, social media, computer games, alcohol, porn, drugs, sports, various social activities, music concerts, over work, and so on. These distractions keep you from feeling and seeing what is happening inside you and around you with others and with the world at large at this time of collapse.

The next questions are these.

1. *What is your own contribution* to the anger, reaction, and confusion going on in your personal environment relative to the political, social, and consuming news and distractions that surround you every day?
2. *What choices are you making* that contribute to your mental and emotional environment by perhaps conditioning you to be swept up and consumed by the negativity of friends, family, work, and the area of the world, country, and home place that surround you?

The last set of questions has you examine how much you are influenced and conditioned by your beliefs, thoughts, emotions, people, media, and situations that surround you every moment of your day and night. It also has you consider how you are cutting yourself off from your inner life, rather than creating positive actions and energy to give to people and situations around you. We want you to examine the people and groups with whom you associate. Ask yourself whether they support positive awareness or foster negative reactions and thereby cause you to separate from people and situations around you, either out of fear or anger or some other feeling state.

Do take these questions and your reflections seriously because in truth these enquiries will determine the immediate conditions you will face in this rapidly exploding and changing local and worldwide chaos. More importantly, these questions can help you discover the potential of your capacity and capability to contribute to a radical transformation of your perception and reality, or not. Facing these questions and issues will enable you to live and move through these chaotic times without fear. You will also find true inner and outer safety, and move within an amazing flow of energy to assist others as they confront conditions that seem overpowering to them. Finally, trust that we are with you, helping you confront and be open to these questions and conditions. Keep coming back to these questions and reflections again and again. We will inwardly prompt you to do so. Let us now continue our discussion.

The times ahead are the times now! In other places we've described, and others also have described, that the year 2016 was a negative turning point in countries all over the world. This is in political, social, and environmental conditions that would rapidly accelerate the chaos, beginning in the 2020s. In the early 2020s, massive upheaval, particularly in the environment, will be devastating around the world. Earthquakes, volcanic eruptions, and massive storms will wipe out cities and crops. There will be eruptions of gasses in the Arctic that are ten times more dangerous to the environment than the carbon produced by coal, oil, and natural gas. This Arctic gas will cause extreme temperature changes, which will make it more difficult to live in many areas of the world. The combination of carbons and permafrost gasses will create temperatures so high that humans and animals will no longer be able to live in vast parts of the world. Diseases of all kinds will begin to sweep the planet and there will be little ability to stop them.

To face all of this will demand a different kind of strength and courage, and an inner kindling of a new awareness. The first two parts of this book are to help you with this inner preparation. Again, we do not tell you these things to either scare you or to traumatize you. In a very real sense, if you are reading this, you already know or sense the magnitude of what is transpiring around you.

Your work and preparation are to release the fear of your ego tapestry and learn to listen and act from a place of inner knowledge, awareness, and guidance. If you sense a condition or environment that would be negative or destructive to you and to those you Love, you can be guided to a place of safety and support for your needs.

Now is the time to be very serious and committed to your inner awareness and generate a different perception of reality than what most people around you are immersed within. When we look from outside your time and space, we see great suffering, indifference, and massive social control of populations around the world to try to respond to this collapse. Authoritarians and militaries will tend to rule the world. Given the massive number of nuclear bombs already in existence, the potential of a massive nuclear event is very possible. This event would wipe out millions of people and leave vast sections of the earth uninhabitable due to radiation. The timing of all these events will be governed by millions of individual choices moving things to one climax or another. If you don't have an inner guidance system, then things may be very difficult for you.

Now, let us also say that this collapse of civilization into chaos can pave the way for a new species to emerge on the planet. You, yes, you are on the planet at this time to help foster a higher frequency of human species that lives from the inner world of heart-mind energy. The heart energy practices we've provided will enable you to both survive and thrive through this time of endings and new beginnings. We will describe more about this in another section.

Enough now of apparent doom and gloom. Yes, you all will face challenging times ahead, but you can be a healer, a leader, or a companion to those who are struggling, by awakening your own gifts, inner knowledge, and experience in order to be part of the pathway to the emergence of a new world. During this difficult period of time you are in, you will grow, evolve, and discover talents and powers you never knew you had. Please know that if you are reading this book, we will be present to support and guide you through these challenging times. Simply call to us and we will be present to you. This time of challenge will actually be a liberating time for you if you are willing to surrender your fear, let go, and trust the inner landscape of your own mind and heart.

As you live more and more in your heart without fear, you will find like-minded people to create an envelope of peace and healing in and around you.

> Now is the time to be very serious and committed to your inner awareness and generate a different perception of reality than what most people around you are immersed within.

Practicing in Pairs

To this end, the basic practice we would urge you to do daily is select one practice from the five pillars of Love and one practice from the five foundation stones of daily living and pair them together and practice both with strong intent for one week. At the end of the week write what you learned from pairing these practices. The next week pair two others and practice them together. Write your learning at the end of that week. Continue to do this week in and week out. We will be working with you to support your commitment and intent.

This practice and reflection done with dedication and our support will not only release the tapestry threads but open the portal of Love within you. It will also activate your inner gifts such as healing, telepathy, looking into the future, feeling changes in weather patterns, activating inner timing for action and movement for safety, finding food, and much more. You will need all these capabilities and more in the days and years ahead, and these gifts are what will sprout the new human that we will speak about in the last section.

Please practice for your own sake, for your loved ones' sake, and for those in your sphere of influence. Know that we will support, help, and encourage your gifts.

> This practice and reflection done with dedication and our support will not only release the tapestry threads but open the portal of Love within you.

The Meaning of the Planet's Environmental Changes

Understanding the Second Challenge

*S*hould we begin now with the second section? I appreciate the information you've given so far. You've indicated that we face many challenges. What are these challenges?

Yes, David, but first we would speak of your personal challenges as we described the challenges to the reader in the last section. We would like you to include this at the beginning of this section as we believe it will help the reader to understand your challenges as well as theirs.

Remember, you tend to perceive, intuit, and understand the larger elements and dimensions of this period of civilization collapse. But your emotional stance is still not firm within you. You too must consider the questions we posed and the practices we suggested in the opening discussion. The tone of the message in that section is that, given the rapidity of collapse at all levels of individual, social, political, and environmental conditions, you must get very serious about your inner preparation. We ask you, in the same way we are asking the reader who will work with this material. Because the time toward growing chaos is short, you must work with your emotions and feelings, and also your intellect. Consistent practice is vital for you.

On the walk in the silence of the woods today, you felt a fear come over you. You felt vulnerable and had anxiety of being alone and wondering what you would do if someone attacked you in that place. That experience demonstrates that you are not ready to operate at a higher level of conscious awareness when fast moving threats appear to you. Are you willing to open yourself to being killed if that were your destiny in any given moment? Your fear of death is still lodged deep within you. This is one of your key challenges.

We trust that you will strengthen your intent and be serious about the material and practices in these four sections. So, let us now begin.

In this section we want to focus on the meaning, purpose, and learning that the environmental changes occurring on the planet now will accelerate in the near future.

Your earth has always had small to great changes of its environment over hundreds of thousands of years. You have had ice ages covering most of Europe and North America within the last fifteen thousand years. Sixty-five million years ago when the asteroid hit the Yucatan Peninsula, all mammals less than a foot or so in length did not survive. Many times, massive volcanic explosions brought a darkening of the planet for years, killing off many species of animal and plant life. We could go on describing many, many more of these changes of great magnitude, but many of you reading this are well aware of these events and more. We give this sampling to indicate that your planet has gone through enormous environmental chaos and imbalance in its past, influencing its process of natural evolution.

What is significant about this period of environmental change is the result of human activity. For example, during the middle of the eighteen hundreds the human population of the planet was approximately one billion souls. Humans were spread out over many continents. That was the acceleration of the industrial revolution. In a little over a hundred and fifty years, the planet now supports over eight billion humans, which in itself is a significant planet-wide stressor. The rise in the earth's temperature since the middle 1800s is increasing to a threatening level. This is the result of industrialization based on the discovery and usage of oil, which produces carbons that pollute the atmosphere. This pollution holds in the heat and kills off people, animals, forests, jungles, and it breaks up the intricate inner play between the various elements of sun, water, air, and earth to keep the planet in a natural balance.

Again, most of you know and understand that these forces of climate change, overpopulation, and habitat destruction, plus military confrontation, nuclear threat, and inner cultural belief warfare are destroying your world and your possibility to bring about real creative and positive change going forward. Metaphorically, you are stuck at the edge of a cliff with nowhere to go.

The culture that we Three came from thousands of years ago is an example of this cliff edge. Our civilization existed before the tectonic plates separated in the now Indian Ocean and Pacific Ocean region and were still connected as part of a huge land mass. That period in the earth's history comprised horrific destruction as the land plates came apart and great land masses sunk into the newly formed oceans. Over time, as earthquakes and volcanic activity progressed, our civilization faced challenging conditions that were similar to what you face today. People like those in your governmental, scientific, technological, social, and political systems came into conflict with each other and would not recognize the coming doom. The combined thought forms of negativity, power, control, and greed of this mind net produced a response in the earth to create massive volcanic and earthquake destruction.

This destroyed our society. There were many people, however, like ourselves who learned in the earlier development of our culture that earth life was a training ground to develop high levels of conscious awareness and mind-heart energy skills. The growing impending destruction of the very ground we lived upon, as well as our collapsing civilization, spurred us on to transcend our bodies and live consciously in a dimension above the third dimension of this earth plane where this destruction was forming.

Our purpose was then, as it is with you today, to assist human learning to transcend and live "above" the toxic and negative existence you live within. This does not mean you will suddenly transcend to another dimension. Although that inner pulse of transcending your own ego structure is the work that is calling you, that greater transcending requires great intention, practice, and skill. What we've been providing you with is the basic groundwork for your conscious evolution. "Living above" means developing your energy capabilities and your perception, and releasing your ego tapestry so that you can access the higher energy functions. Learning these things is not just something interesting to do. The breakdown of the earth—including its social systems and fundamental values—requires that if you are to survive, grow, and evolve you must take on this work of energetic development.

The meaning then of this time of civilization collapse and environmental rebalancing will give you the opportunity to speed up your spiritual, psychological, and psychic evolution.

Whenever this planet becomes imbalanced in any way, there is an innate reaction to reharmonize the evolutionary process. The earth itself always remains, even when it appears to be devastated. What is happening now with the planet is a desperate "shaking" to dislodge the mental, emotional, and negative activity that humans have created. This worldwide mind net of negativity, greed, and destruction is creating this wider reaction of the earth, which incidentally, for those who are ready to respond, opens up the channels of the heart to evolve. At some level, reading this indicates you are opening your heart channel. You live in the midst of this planet's upheaval. The reality is that the planet works in tandem with humans and other beings at a spiritual, non-physical level in times of environmental collapse to develop another evolutionary direction. That direction is not at the outer physical level. The planet, the spirit energy entity of the earth, takes care of the physical "shaking" up of the environment for rebalance. Humans who realize that they must speed up inner development are in resonance with the spirit of the earth to evolve their species. Individuals and groups are using this tension of destruction to evolve themselves rapidly. These people, indeed groups all over the planet who are responding in this way, are experiencing new flows of energy and accepting new gifts emerging within them. These individuals and groups are not trying to change events, but rather to change their own course and that of human evolution.

We will describe more about this evolution at the end of this third part. The question we ask you now, however, is this: Are you using the collapse to transform yourself and further the evolution of your species?

The meaning then of this time of civilization collapse and environmental rebalancing will give you the opportunity to speed up your spiritual, psychological, and psychic evolution.

Do you understand the impact on you of the nature of the force, the energy, the incredible tension of events that surround you? Do you understand that the events playing out in the world—both negative and positive—are all assuming their part to evolve humans toward a different consciousness? Also in your inner calling is for you to play your part to create a different way to live and evolve this planet's destiny by consciously becoming part of the vast multi-universe system.

Survival and consciousness go together to produce evolution. Through its relentless technology, overpopulation, and constant destructive warfare, your species has created a very complex environment and structure that can no longer sustain itself.

Complexity is causing your destruction as a species. Only consciousness development, along with individual and collective use of the energy of Love as we've described it in previous sections, will enable the species to reach an apex of evolution. If reached, this apex of evolution can create harmony, freedom, and the ability to stop and transcend this human societal predicament where death, destruction, and ideologies trap the mind and heart to repeat itself from society to society and from generation to generation.

To summarize what we have been describing to you: millions of choices externally and internally by humans have brought the species to this critical point in its life cycle of evolution and development. No specific idea, structure, or leader brought you to this nexus moment. You are witnessing a huge change of state in the species. Either humans will release these convoluted patterns of consciousness built around greed, power, and reckless control (of other humans, of nature, and of the interwoven systems that sustain life balance), or the species will cease to exist. Of all the civilizations that have risen and fallen on this planet, this current collapse may end the human experiment here. Or it may jump the gap and create a different type of human and a different planet. You, who are reading this in this moment, are part of that choice. Toward this end of making a personal choice, we ask you to consider the following.

Practice

We would like you to take on a daily practice in order to explore and decide on the choices before you.

In response to the result of your civilization's complexity and outward mode of expression, we would like you to examine daily the choices you are making in every part of your life. There are of course small to large choices you make every day. These are simple ones such as what you choose to eat; checking messages on your smart phone; watching different programs on TV; talking with family members; listening, watching, or reading the news. Or, the choice may be to meditate, do spiritual practices. Other choices you make could be to compare and judge yourself and others, get angry at the government or politicians, volunteer to help people, drink alcohol, take drugs, focus on different forms of entertainment, be fair and honest at your work, socialize with friends, react with fear toward people you call enemies, get angry, get sad. The list of daily choices goes on and on.

All we want you to do with this practice is to observe what choices you are making, without changing any of them or judging yourself for your choices.

We suggest that at the beginning of this observing exercise that you set a time before going to sleep to review your day and remember the choices you made throughout the day. There is no judgement about your choices or about anything you did or didn't do during the day.

If you do this practice for a couple of weeks you will begin to notice that you will be more conscious of your choices as you actually make them. *To be the observer is the first step in making different kinds of choices.* If you are serious about doing the energetic practices we've given in this book, your observations and the natural awareness of choices will begin to naturally and automatically change what, how, and why you will make different choices to bring you into a different relationship of harmony with others around you and with the spirit of the earth itself.

This simple practice of observing without self-judgement will not only teach you about your choices, but also teach you how to be free. Learning how not to judge yourself for your choices and shifting naturally to different choices will help you learn to experience true awareness, release more of your ego tapestry, and generate greater evolution of your true nature.

> **This simple practice of observing without self-judgement will not only teach you about your choices, but also teach you how to be free.**

The Spiritual Meaning of Endings and Beginnings

Understanding the Third Challenge

This third section focuses on the spiritual meaning of endings and beginnings. We choose this title because the outer world clearly appears to be ending and there is hope in many people that somehow there can be a new beginning. If we stay focused on all the current chaos and confusion, things do not appear hopeful. In fact, many scientists and technologists in your world believe you need an escape plan for the human race, as the potential for total destruction appears certain to them. The escape plan is to put humans on Mars so that somehow the human species will still have the potential to survive. The chances of that happening, however, are very small, given how rapidly the effects of massive climate change are occurring.

Things in your world may appear drastic, but a new beginning for humanity will start here on the earth not on another planet.

So, what do we mean by "spiritual" endings and beginnings?

All your spiritual teachers and mystics throughout the ages have always said there will be a great cataclysm that will shake the world to its core. This warning in the Vedic tradition was known as the Kali Yuga. In the Christian Bible, the Prophet John in the Book of Revelations saw the Four Horsemen of the Apocalypse. Hopi and many indigenous teachings in the northern and southern hemispheres spoke of these end times. Throughout the ages, many people and groups sensed, envisioned, and proclaimed an apocalyptic period of massive calamity on the earth. All these traditions and prophetic visions speak of a cleansing of the world and the return of the true world and the true human.

> **When a major ending of the "world" is spoken of, it is also to reveal a new pathway for humanity. The pathway, however, is not apparent in the midst of the ending turmoil and destruction.**

When a major ending of the "world" is spoken of, it is also to reveal a new pathway for humanity. The pathway, however, is not apparent in the midst of the ending turmoil and destruction. All these traditions speak of old souls arriving at this time; that is beings who come into the world at this time to prepare others for the new pathway and the new beginning of human kind. These old souls, we would say, are humans who have awakened to the consciousness of their true nature and the knowledge of the energies of Love. They have come to be the teachers and guides for those who can hear and perceive a new path.

You must recognize, however, that the path of a new beginning is only seen as far as one's pure consciousness can see. Many will see a few steps ahead, but the old souls teach that in reality you make up the new path as you discover it with others. This seeing of the path individually and together is learning how to step out of time and space and be able to perceive what lies ahead.

In the Foundation Stone known as Release of Old Patterns, we gave a practice of going into the past and into the future to forgive, heal, and change the direction of the time-space map. Without clear initiation by a wise soul teacher, it is difficult to fully step out of time-space and clearly view events in the past and future. The Release practice focused on attempting to look seven generations into the past and seven generations into the future. Some of you doing that practice may have developed the skills to go forward 175 years to see the consequences of the choices being made today. To see clearly is also to perceive the innumerable choices that are made each step on that time path. From looking back 175 years, you will come to see the results of the myriad of negative and unconscious choices that have created your world today. The value of that practice is to realize that going forward and back one can begin to realize the magnitude of many individual and collective choices.

> You must recognize, however, that the path of a new beginning is only seen as far as one's pure consciousness can see. Many will see a few steps ahead, but the old souls teach that in reality you make up the new path as you discover it with others. This seeing of the path individually and together is learning how to step out of time and space and be able to perceive what lies ahead.

To speak of spiritual endings, we need to discuss the notion of karma. The simple understanding of karma is that choices made and actions taken have consequences. The notion of karma is that it is not one set of actions that produce consequences, but many, many actions done both consciously and unconsciously that result in some perceived consequence. We suggest that what is important about the idea of karma is that it is a web that can never be figured out or explained. It is like the tapestry of your ego that has a multitude of threads woven together creating patterns within patterns. To release the tapestry of your ego takes much concentrated intent and openness to your karmic conditions to transform and release the "I" that dominates your separation from reality. The consequence of any karmic action is it reduces one's experience to a narrow view of existence. The function of karma is to contract reality for a person and shut off the experience of expansion and connection to all of existence and, therefore, develop the self-constructed ego tapestry.

At the beginning of one's life when you leave your mother's womb there is an experience of abandonment and separation. This is both a psychological and spiritual experience for the baby. The challenge of the experience in returning to the human realm is to be cut away from infinity, from the awareness that one is held in oneness and completeness. The birth trauma is the first karmic lesson. One has returned not as a blank slate but as a being who has brought conditions from previous incarnations that provide one's healing and opportunity to discover and awaken back to the infinite reality. Each choice, action, and response both in the child and those around the child will create mutual projections of Love, trust, pain, doubt, and a host of other characteristics that are taken into the soul. These projections of the child onto the world and the projections from parents and others onto the child will determine the inner and outer conditions of the pathway to a new beginning. Each of you has experienced this process. For some it has appeared easy, for others very difficult. Through the birth and the projection process (that is ongoing throughout life), the old karma you have brought into this life along with the inner gift that needs to be awakened to find your inner path are the conditions that form your life experience in this moment.

Most of you have struggled both to heal the karma that you arrived with in this life and to discover what your true gift is that sets you on your unique path. The good news in this dark period is that you are in the fundamental inner and outer tension that can awaken and open awareness and understanding of the karma that needs to be released and the realization of the unique gifts that you were destined to express at this time. It is for this reason that you chose to be living on the planet at this time. The endings and beginnings of an old world dying and the possibility of a new humanity emerging reveal the spiritual reason for your being here at this moment of time.

Each of you has this spiritual opportunity to awaken and embark on a new path in your life. We believe that any conscious being will open to this new path if they are willing to release the old karma and open to the new possibility within them. In this release of karma is a pathway of inner freedom and expansion to the true nature of existence.

> **Each of you has this spiritual opportunity to awaken and embark on a new path in your life.**

We see in you as you read now that there is the remembrance, the struggle, the longing, and the doubt that your life could really be different. You fear that you will never discover your gift or the true meaning of your life. But the inner spark that is creating these ego machinations knows the truth, wants the truth, and is eager to be liberated both from your past and from an uncertain and seemingly dark future. It is hard to dissuade you from these feelings until you directly begin to experience this release from your prison of inner darkness.

> **Remember, when we speak of karma, we are using that term as shorthand for the results and consequences of your actions, thoughts and intents from this life or other existences.**

Remember, the darkness is not real. The darkness is the cover of your ego tapestry keeping you locked into a false representation of your true potential.

People living at this time will die because of unreleased karma. Others will try to escape the pain of despair and depression through a multitude of compensating consumptions only to return to some existence to try to learn the truth about themselves. Have compassion for your pain and struggle, and have compassion for the millions around the world who chose conditions coming into this life that are beyond your comprehension. Be grateful that your karma brought you into conditions that provide an opportunity for release, freedom, and the opportunity to not only create endings, release, and forgiveness of yourself, but a new beginning to help choose a new pathway for humanity.

Practice

Our practice for you is to take a notebook and write down all the challenges you've encountered in your life. We recommend that you sit and relax yourself, meditate, or do whatever quiets your body before you begin this exercise. The intent of the relaxation is to settle your body as well as your mind so that you can remember from your heart. It is your heart that carries your karmic lessons, both from when you were born and through the years since to this moment in your life.

Remember, when we speak of karma, we are using that term as shorthand for the results and consequences of your actions, thoughts, and intents from this life or other existences.

After sitting in a quiet period of relaxation, begin to write about your life. Write with a pen or pencil rather than type on a computer as handwriting opens the memory gates more deeply. The physicality of the body-mind-heart relationship will bring to mind the remembrances that are karmically important for you. As an example, allow these to arise: thoughts and images of your family and friends; your successes and failures; the misunderstandings, hurts, and arguments; and the people you cared for and those you disliked. The point here is to let your heart recall whatever "needs" to come up at this time.

> **YOU are the answer to every question in your life.**

Throughout the entire time you spend writing down each event, person, or situation say, "Thank You" and touch your heart with your free hand. Both writing and touching your heart activate body-mind-heart awareness. Write and give thanks until you begin to feel inward release and silence within. When this occurs put down your pen, close your journal or paper, and now sit in silence, focusing your attention on your heart. Your mind may wander. Just gently bring your mind back to the feeling and energy growing in your heart.

As your heart energy gets stronger, ask your heart, "What is my gift and what is my path in the world?" Don't try to think what it is. Rest gently in the question itself. Don't expect an answer mentally. You may get images or feelings or seemingly nothing. Most of all, don't let yourself get caught up in doubt. You may have to repeat this exercise a number of times. When you realize your heart gift and your pathway, you will immediately feel and experience clarity, knowing, and trust to open to the gift and explore and be guided in your path.

The reality is that each of you came into this life with a gift and each of you has a unique path to express that gift. For some of you, this exercise may simply confirm your gift and reveal your path. For others of you, in the days that follow, be open to the answer to your questions as they naturally arise in the circumstances of your daily activity. *Be without expectations of an "answer." You are the answer.*

Trust that both the gift and the path are coming to conscious awareness through your daily experience. It is not at the point of doing the exercise that you discover the answer. The remembering, the constant thankfulness, and the heart centeredness are what enable you to be conscious of living the answer that is you.

> **The reality is that each of you came into this life with a gift and each of you has a unique path to express that gift.**

YOU are the answer to every question in your life.

The great challenge is to trust that you will live out those answers. The living out of the question and answer is the magic of your life. The magic is the synchronicities, the improbable events, the people, and the astounding experiences that come to you and suddenly manifest without your doing anything. Your answers will come from encounters with physical and non-physical beings, with spirits of trees and water, with birds and rocks, with the sun and stars. You will be thinking of someone and they will appear to give you the next step of discovery. **Trust that there is no one way through which you will discover your true gift, your true path, and the experience of genuine awakening to the world and the greater existence.**

In all your questioning we will be with you. Call on us. We will help you. We are present in this world to support you.

One Final Note

Every human is valuable, important, and attempting to meet the conditions of completing their endings and discovering new beginnings. Be available to whomever comes into your life. This doesn't mean you bring everyone into your intimate circle. *Availability* means that each being at some point in your existence touched and touches your life, and that can increase a heart response from you. Your availability to the cashier at the store, the person you dislike at work, your child who is difficult and moody, the policeman who gave you a speeding ticket, and so on are part of your path and a means for you to express your gift.

Your availability is your openness of heart and the giving of your heart energy and feelings as blessings to each being whom you touch and who touches you.

The energy of heart Love is always the medicine everyone needs.

Be blessed in that heart medicine.

The Promise of a New World, a New Pattern of Living, and the Awakening of the Truly Human

We begin now with the last section of this part of the book. We titled this section about discovering a new world, a new pattern of living together, and even the awakening of the "truly human."

It may seem that we are speaking to the future in this title. In one sense we are; however, we are also helping you understand and claim for yourself in this present moment that you can both discover and live in a new world of experience, where relations with others are more heart-based and where you can awaken to your true humanity and be your gift to the world in this lifetime.

We hope that you've begun to realize through the first three sections of this last part that the gift of these end times is a great opportunity to be released from the mundane consciousness of daily life. The threat of survival and the fear of great change on the planet are part of creating the energy for you to awaken to the creative potential within you and the possibility of bringing people together in your local environment. This will be the opportunity to establish communities of trust, Love, creativity, mutual support, safety, and protection.

We say *protection* not as a survival notion, but rather how to foresee and take actions that permit enclaves of groups to nurture children and old folks to help guide this journey through a true evolution on the planet.

The challenge of forming communities will be difficult. The old forms of structure, leadership, and control won't work; they won't survive the immense challenges of the near term. There will be many forms of groups arising and evolving into communities. These new communities will have a different focus and structure. *These communities that will arise will need to be guided by wise women. This does not mean that men will not have leadership roles. They will. However, men will need to be tempered by the feminine energy that is the "womb" for birthing a different kind of community structure and environment.* It does not mean that a council of women makes all the decision and choices. Rather, the women will hold a context of energy and conscious awareness in which a foundation of Love, support, intuition, wisdom, and foresight can help to both support the community and provide checks and balances on the choices and actions and on the aggression that men so easily rush toward.

> **We say *protection* not as a survival notion, but rather how to foresee and take actions that permit enclaves of groups to nurture children and old folks to help guide this journey through a true evolution on the planet.**

There will be men as well as women who will be seers, healers, ceremonial leaders, teachers, growers of food, builders, and much more. All will be needed to sustain a self-contained community. These types of communities are already spread around the world and under the radar, so to speak. However, as the world begins to darken and fall apart at the social and environmental levels, there will be more and more of these arising. Many of the communities that have already formed are learning the strengths, pitfalls, and daily challenges of creating and living in communal relationship.

Communities will break apart when males and females fail to release their ego tapestry and vie for control and dominance. Communities will fail when they do not establish feminine energy at their center. Communities will fail when there is not a fundamental growth and teaching of heart-level development. Communities will fail when there is not a mix of the very young and the old.

The older adults will need to discover the gifts of their wisdom and inner experience. The young will need to be nourished by the entire community and not just by their birth parents. Multiple individuals nurturing children are needed in order to mitigate the normal separation and abandonment that comes from being born. By the common responsibility of many adults caring for children and teenagers, and by the wisdom of the old watching for the gifts that young people have and encouraging them, a new seed of the truly human can sprout. *The children, the growing adults, and the aged provide the means together of being containers of the new human.*

In your lives, you will not see the new humans, but you will see the beginning of their birth. With all the trials and challenges that will come internally within the community as well as the incalculable threats from the external environment, these communities will be the incubators for a potentially new human experiment.

Individuals here and there throughout the world will incarnate with powers, knowledge, and the ability to awaken souls. They will quickly move through regions, encouraging the coming together of communities and tribes of communities of people. These individuals will be healers, teachers, and wisdom carriers who can rebalance and guide individuals in new directions. They can help to strengthen communities to align with other groups.

Most importantly, they will help release old beliefs and ideological systems that keep individuals, groups, and communities in old patterns. The old patterns will not stand in the awakening and the tide of new energies that are emerging in the world.

Whenever a planet of beings goes through the conditions of your journey of three-dimensional ego experience and cultural collapse, evolution must accelerate. Help will arrive. Beings like us are called to come from infinite awareness to be present and supportive of the potential evolution that can emerge here. We are not superior to you. We have gone through thousands of incarnations and arrived at the point of potential liberation in the same way that you face with the massive conflagration that confronts you on your planet today.

We have come to support you. Many beings like ourselves are present, challenging you to energize your heart, providing insight and information, teaching and providing guidance, and supporting individuals and groups of people. What is important for you to know is that we can teach, encourage, and support you, but we cannot control, dominate, or take away your choices, decisions, and learning, or your individual and collective destinies. These worldwide calamities provide an acceleration for growth, development, and breakthroughs both for individuals and the potential of a new level of human evolution. There are scientists, police, teachers, doctors, healers, professors, carpenters, inventors, mothers, couples, and religious figures—all types of people—who are part of this growing potential.

You who are reading this are part of the harbingers. It is those of you who feel the impulse of awakening within and realizing your gifts are emerging and are challenged by the circumstances of the times who move in new directions with groups of people who resonate at the same energetic level. You are willing to use group energy in community to expand and express a new awareness in the process of daily living. At the core of this awareness is the feeling, insight, and understanding that you and others are being called to be the seeds of a new humanity that will break the stranglehold on delaying the emergence of humans that will cross the gap from the old human to the new one.

Given what we described we suggest a practice for you to explore these comments we have made.

Practice

Our practice for this section is simple. We encourage you to first examine within yourself if this is the time for you to be part of a community of support, protection, and spiritual encouragement that has the willingness to challenge you to grow your gifts and awaken to who you truly are.

How will you know you are ready to be part of something much larger than yourself? You may already be part of some group. It may be a service organization in your community. It may be a church or some kind of spiritual group. It may be a group that does yoga or a group that in some way is developing your body, mind, and heart through meditation, chanting, or chi gong. These kinds of groups and activities, among many we did not name, provide a starting point for your considerations and exploration of the larger question of your commitment to a living community.

> When meeting with a new group, notice if you feel guarded or on edge with the people, purpose, and functioning of the group. Observe the attitudes and relationships with the people in the group and whether they "synch" with you through conversation, feeling, and how your body is responding, being with them. Most importantly do you feel challenged by the individuals and the purpose of the group in a positive way so that this community of people would help you grow and open to your awakening?

We suggest that you make a list of the group(s) you participate in routinely. If you are not part of a group, consider what kind of group might interest you. If you are currently in a group(s) or not, sit in the quiet regularly so you can begin to formulate what kind of group would help you take the next step in your life. Whatever arises in you let yourself explore the possibilities by examining the group(s) you are in, or if not in a group, find a group and attend so you can determine your inner resonance of your being to the group.

The first part of this exercise is to increase your inner resonance capacity for a group.

For those not in a group currently your intent at the beginning of exploring a group is not to join, rather it is to explore the resonance between the group and yourself. *Resonance is the sense of being welcomed or not at your heart level.* When meeting with a new group, notice if you feel guarded or on edge with the people, purpose, and functioning of the group. Observe the attitudes and relationships with the people in the group and whether they "synch" with you through conversation, feeling, and how your body is responding, being with them. Most importantly do you feel challenged by the individuals and the purpose of the group in a positive way so that this community of people would help you grow and open to your awakening?

For those already in a group(s), reexamine your resonance to a particular group in the way we explained above. You may choose to exit from some group(s) or reinforce your relationship to other group(s).

For those already in group(s) and for those exploring a new group, understand that the group does not need to be perfect. *What you are exploring is a heart feeling and an inner knowing.* If you attempt to continue with the group that you are already in or if you are seeking a new group, your decision to be part of it or not needs to be based on something other than preference. As we've emphasized, your key instrument of decision-making is the focus on your inner resonance and a radar of genuine heart feelings about the group on your part. If you are keyed in to the resonance within you, your intuition will give you the yes or no.

We recommend for those of you who are already part of a group or groups, do the same conscious resonance testing. There may be groups you need to leave but have felt reluctant to do so. There may be other groups of which you've been on the fringes, but you haven't committed to yet and you realize that the group is more in alignment with you.

As we've said in the last section, the choices you make are not ultimately through thinking but through your heart resonance. At the mental level, a group may not make sense to you, but the heart feeling, intuition, and insight about your own needs will guide you. *Remember this: just as humans evolve, so do groups when they are guided by heart energy.*

> Your key instrument of decision-making is the focus on your inner resonance and a radar of genuine heart feelings about the group on your part. If you are keyed in to the resonance within you, your intuition will give you the yes or no.

First Step

This first step in the practice, then, is to explore your resonance with a group or groups that is in the sphere of your daily life. Most of you reading this are not part of a committed living community. We realize for most of you that a commitment to a living, engaged, stand-alone community is not possible at this point in your life. The exploration at this stage is to begin to learn what kind of group can prepare you for taking the jump to a living community when that is needed for you, and for your family if you have one.

Second Step

For some of you who are already in a group that meets the criterion of heart resonance, you may need to initiate several conversations: one that challenges the group to have more heart-centered interaction about individual relationships with one another; one about the values guiding the group; one about the purpose for the outward service of the group; and another about the level of inner and outer development that is fostered or not by the group. This can often be a challenging discussion and requires a compassionate and open presence for others to hear your concerns and requests.

You may have to engage in individual conversations before a group discussion. Remember the purpose of these kinds of conversation is to explore for yourself what are the challenges working and living with people in a group setting. Your intent is that of gratitude for the group, compassion for yourself and others, as well as courage and a trust that, whatever the outcome of this type of conversation, *it will take time for individuals and a group to "upgrade" their resonance and purpose together.*

Third Step

The third step is for some of you that may want to start a new group.

If you feel an inner calling to start a new group that embodies the concerns and issues we've outlined, we can provide a few guidelines.

What starting a new group means is first knowing that you have an inner calling to create a group and inner guidance of the purpose and structure of the group. However, understand that you are being called as an "initiator," not necessarily as the leader of a group. Being the initiator requires a deep resonance of commitment within you. Without a resonance of commitment to the unknown and what you will learn, be careful about initiating a group. This may not be the right time; your guidance to want to initiate may be waiting on a certain time for bringing together those who have the same resonance as you.

Again, an initiator of a group is not necessarily the leader of a group. An initiator carries the energetic impulse that can draw others to the vision, to the promise of what the group or project is about. Leadership of a group goes beyond the initiation and resonance to the manifestation of structure, problem solving, and all the issues a true leader must hold as the steward of the group. You may hold the position of both initiator and leader for the new group, but you must watch carefully and examine yourself as to whether indeed you have the strength, capacities, experience, and capability to also be the functional leader. As an initiator, if you recognize you are not the functional leader, you must be in a high level of resonance with the leader, and the leader with you.

As an initiator you draw people toward a common resonance of ideas, purposes, insights, forms of service, or whatever is being sparked within you. Recognize that this initiator impulse is an activation of your gift that you may not have realized before. An inner spark is what often activates our true gift. If the notion to initiate a particular group purpose and focus is your work, it will take time, commitment to keep going, and inner guidance to formulate what, why, where, and how the intent of the group can be manifested and communicated to others.

You can initiate the purpose and form of the new group to others, but the resonance and feeling and intention will either pull people to explore with you or not. Remember, it is your inner calling, guidance, and resonance to the spark of creating the group that is calling you, not the ideas or purpose or organization that call a group into being. You do not need to know everything. Just be alert to the inner nudges and situations that emerge and guide you.

For any of you examining the possibility of group creation, the challenge is not judgement and attachment to your views, but a willingness to take action and to let go to those who also want to contribute to the creation. Group life will always be in growth and evolution of mutual creation if individuals are in resonance and contributing their gifts and abilities. Always the willingness to let go is what opens space for mutual resonance, participation, contribution, and creativity.

> **Doing the practices of the Energy Teachings can provide a foundation and resonance that will help you to survive and thrive in ways you can't imagine.**

These three discussions about group involvement represent the first learning phase of group resonance and development. The groups you are in, want to be in, or want to create are preparation and learning situations for the survive-and-thrive communities that you may become involved in. An important question is, Will any group for which you begin a deeper commitment and resonance become a "living in community" group for you?

As conditions worsen in society and the environment, will you be able to establish or be part of "living in community" that would create a safe place for you and your family? Do your current neighbors, community, and surrounding area provide the potential for self-sufficiency, growing food, water, protection from the breakdown of normal structures, governance and societal laws? Does your locale meet the challenges of major climate events that will affect your surrounding environment?

> **Will any group for which you begin a deeper commitment and resonance become a "living in community" group for you?**

In answering these questions, you may consider seeking other areas and communities that would be more suitable for living through major changes. Moving is always a challenge. It requires seeking inner guidance. If you have a family, it is necessary to align with your partner and even your children about leaving. Your views may seem too radical for them to act on in the way you believe and feel. Choices like this cannot come from reacting from fear, or from some mental view and beliefs, but from where your path is taking you, and the gifts and direction of your life. It will be your resonance, Love, and caring that you have in order for you to align together or not. The question will always be this: "Did I jump too soon or wait too long? "

> Again, we say to you who are reading this book, doing the practices of the Energy Teachings can provide a foundation and resonance that will help you to survive and thrive in ways you can't imagine.

Choosing to become part of a "living in community" in order to "survive and thrive," one must be careful and serious about the practices of seeking within, releasing the ego tapestry, confronting one's own death, and trusting the purpose for which you came into this life. Your destiny may be to stay where you are living and be of service, caring, and compassion for those around you. Everyone will have their own purpose in these times, fulfilling their own karma and soul destiny. Your life's gifts and path are the road you and everyone must choose to fulfill.

Today, in your life there are lessons to learn, miracles to be experienced, relationships to be nourished, and new ways of creativity to express through you. The opportunity of these times before you, before everyone, is the challenge to awaken to the truth of who you really are. It is to awaken to your deepest gifts and express them and thereby discover an amazing path of learning that leads you to ultimate reality. Whether this comes from being in a particular "living in community" or not, this is the ultimate purpose in your life.

Again, we say to you who are reading this book, doing the practices of the Energy Teachings can provide a foundation and resonance that will help you to survive and thrive in ways you can't imagine.

> **There are beings like us from many dimensions who are present now and whom you can call upon. Remember, in our communication we advise, encourage, teach, and support you. That is our role here. We do not make decisions and choices for you. In this earth dimension, you learn to awaken through your own choices and decisions.**

Each of you has guides and teachers who are present for you. Learn to connect with them. There are energy spirits all around you in the earth and sky, in the trees and flowers, in the animals and birds, and in the mountains and seas. You may never see or hear them speak to you, but all beings have consciousness and you will find that you naturally resonate toward different beings. Thank them, honor them, and ask for their assistance in all the ways your life unfolds.

A simple way to begin contact with us or with other teachers, guides, and nature beings is to sit in a quiet and meditative state with a notebook and pen, and ask for us or other beings to be present with you. Formulate a question and begin to write in response to that question.

At first you may believe that nothing special is happening. Or you may feel you are just writing the words because of the thoughts or imagination of your own mind and ego. Remember that we are using your mental and emotional structure to respond to your question.

Each time you doubt, move back into your heart and affirm the trust of your consciousness expanding in a new way, and say the phrase you worked with in Reflection: "I release all thoughts, all memories, all emotions that created my life and my world." Focus that phrase in your head and repeat it several times and then shift your focus to your heart repeating, "Love is my essence, all that I am is Love."

Even in this exercise of making contact with us you are releasing more of the threads of your ego tapestry. Then go back to the writing. Notice as you write that there is a gap between your thoughts and what you are writing. It is in that gap of silence that you are connecting at a deeper level; the flow of the writing, the feeling of connection, will grow. When you lose that gap of feeling, stop, go to your heart, and then continue to write. As with any practice, you are breaking old patterns and creating new ones. In time many of you will not have to write; you may begin to hear the voice and can dialogue in that manner. Others of you will actually see images of what is being communicated to you. No matter in what inner form the communication is occurring at the beginning of your communication practice, we suggest you write down what you are experiencing as that is a grounding process and a way to review what has been communicated to you. Over time it will be a natural process to communicate with the unseen energies and presences that are ever present with you.

There are beings like us from many dimensions who are present now and whom you can call upon. Remember, in our communication we advise, encourage, teach, and support you. That is our role here. We do not make decisions and choices for you. In this earth dimension, you learn to awaken through your own choices and decisions.

Trust yourself, Love yourself, tune in to the inner resonance of the energy frequency of Love. Practice that which will nourish your heart, heal your wounds, and release the tapestry of your ego so that you, yes, you can live in the true nature of who you really are.

> **Trust yourself, Love yourself, tune in to the inner resonance of the energy frequency of Love. Practice that which will nourish your heart, heal your wounds, and release the tapestry of your ego so that you, yes, you can live in the true nature of who you really are.**

Afterword

Dear friends,

You readers who have responded to this material and have worked with the practices, may you realize a new potential to develop the power of heart energy within you.

We affirm again that we have been with you as you've read and attempted to work with the practices. It is the practices of the energies of Love that are most important. In many respects the material, the concepts, and the topics we've provided are less important than that you daily take the time to work with the practices. It is with the energy practices that you can unwind the tapestry of your ego structure, awaken to your true nature, and have the ability to live a life free from fear, doubt, anger, shame, and despair.

> **This work and our approach will speak to some and not to others.**

The forces of nature and the forces of civilization are both crumbling and rebalancing this planet that is home for you. An improbable future reaches out before you, for you as an individual and for humanity. This collapse creates the tension that is needed to develop a new species that can be transformed by the power of Love. How this transformation will occur is being expressed through many beings and in many different ways at this time. This work and our approach will speak to some and not to others.

Many voices are appearing at this time as a counterpoint to the destructiveness of your world. If we speak to you through this material, we encourage you to practice and open yourself in service to others. Our purpose with this material is to encourage you to become both an example and a voice of healing for yourself, your family, friends, and community, and for the many non-human beings on this planet. Nature is your companion and all forms—animals, birds, fishes, trees, the weather, oceans, and rivers—are conscious. They are reaching out to you. Listen, open yourself to them, for they will teach and help you during this difficult time.

Know that you are sustained by the Presence of Consciousness at all levels of existence and this Presence will support you, care for you, and help you in practical ways if you will only reach out and feel and respond to it.

Know that each of you has guides and teachers from beyond this three-dimensional reality, even if you are not conscious of them. Learn to open yourself to the wealth of teaching, support, and caring they can provide to you.

Above all, there is a Force and Presence that encompasses all that we are. You may call it God, the Cosmos, Presence, Light, or by whatever word you choose. This Presence is the Source of all Existence. It is timeless and all encompassing. It is this Presence that you are becoming.

You are entering into a time of direct experience, not one of beliefs. Beliefs come and go in the development of conscious awareness. The pattern of growth and development and service to others is always a process of letting go of old beliefs, attitudes, and behaviors. The times you are in require and provide the means to have an encounter of direct knowing and experience. This direct experience of Presence and reality will be easy for some of you and difficult for others. Know that whatever the conditions and circumstances of your life, both the inward and outward difficulties of your life will accelerate the power of Love to blossom within you.

Throughout this material, we have affirmed that we are actually present with you as you read and practice what we are giving to you. We are not gods; rather we are elder guides and teachers whom you can call upon if you choose. Throughout your history, spiritual teachers have affirmed that you are to ask and you will receive. You each have teachers and guides. Ask them and ask us as you face conditions and opportunities, challenges, and problems. Help is always present for you if you ask.

So, we would request that the last practice for you as you finish this book is to sit in silence now.

1. Use your breath to relax and feel the energy of gratitude rise up from the earth through your body into your heart and then feel the energy of the cosmos flow down through the top of your head into your heart.
2. Breathe into your heart the combined energy that both grounds you and expands you. *This is medicine for your heart*.
3. Continue to sit in this stillness of your heart for a while as you breathe in this combined energy of heaven and earth.
4. In this stillness, ask that heart energy to guide you and show you more clearly your path, your purpose, and the immediate direction of your life.
5. Feel within you the trust and then open your mind and surrender your fears. Know that this asking for direction will unfold

both within your mind and heart and in your environment through other people, circumstances, and encounters with the forces of nature. When you wholeheartedly ask for help, it comes to you.

The key for your life is to continue to let this medicine of your heart guide you and open you to the reality of existence. Sit daily in this stillness of your heart, and all that is destined to come and be expressed in and through you will manifest in beauty, power, creativity, and compassion.

Be at peace, trust your heart, and know you are guided. We are grateful that you are in the world at this time and place.

Acknowledgement

I offer a deep bow of appreciation and gratitude to the Three—Kandin, Jaybar, and Raymar—to you who know only Love—for the years of guidance, teachings, and inner development.

About the Author

David T. Kyle, PhD

From the age of seven, David T. Kyle, PhD, has had a variety of paranormal and initiatory experiences. Throughout the years he has studied and been taught and initiated by several shamanic and gifted spiritual teachers. The shamanic traditions have been the underlying foundation for his life growth and work in the world. As a teacher, consultant, writer, and healer, learning to trust inner guidance and direction have provided the pathway of his life. He has been a writer all his life. Like most writers, he has written both fiction and nonfiction, poetry, short stories, and articles. He considers this work, *Energy Teachings of the Three*, and a forthcoming fiction series titled, The End of History, will help us orient to the challenging times we are in and give us direction and vision. The first book in The End of History series to be published will be called "The Voice."

For further information contact David at www.davidkylenc.com.

Books by the Author

Human Robots & Holy Mechanics:
Reclaiming Our Souls in a Machine World

The adventure of another kind of life and world is beginning to emerge and is growing in many of us. As we choose a different way of living and return to our inner knowing for the truth of what ancient peoples have always seen, we move away from the Machine's consumer-driven world while we are still living in it. Our task is to find out how to be holy mechanics, how to help ourselves as human robots reclaim our souls, particularly as the Machine world begins to break down. The first step is to understand how trapped we are in a mechanized, consumer-driven society. We each need to discover how the corporation economy creates a Machine Culture in which all of us are "oilers" of our spiritual impoverishment. We have been cut off from the sacred and we each need a deeper spiritual initiation. We need also to initiate elder-leaders, establish epiphanic communities, fast from the media, and map the topography of our inner experience to reclaim the sacred in our daily lives and conceive a different future together.

The Four Powers of Leadership:
Presence, Intention, Wisdom, Compassion

Leadership comes to most of us in many forms, from local service organizations, religious communities, and small businesses to corporations with their many layers from managers to the CEO. *The Four Powers of Leadership* will help you understand your leadership style and cultivate the Four Powers for any kind of leadership. Whether you are struggling with leadership issues or simply want to be the best leader you can be, understanding your strengths and weaknesses as a leader will permit you to be more authentic and effective. You will gain an understanding of the gap between personal power (your inherent, innate, leader charisma) and your positional power (the authority vested in your specific position as a leader), and the nature of the Four Powers as a means of bridging this gap. You will also find models and tools to help you cultivate the Four Powers in your own life and become the extraordinary leader you were meant to be.

Made in the USA
Monee, IL
03 May 2021